THE ENTREPRENEUR IN
YOU

THE ENTREPRENEUR IN YOU

CAPITALIZING ON YOUR IDEA

CHARLES KANNANKERIL

Konark Publishers Pvt. Ltd
206, First Floor
Peacock Lane, Shahpur Jat
New Delhi - 110 049
+91-11-4105 5065
india@konarkpublishers.com, us@konarkpublishers.com
www.konarkpublishers.com

Copyright © Charles Kannankeril, 2026

All rights reserved. No part of this book may be reproduced or utilised in any form or by any means, electronic or mechanical, including photocopying, recording, or by any information storage and retrieval system, without prior written permission from the author or the publisher. The views and opinions expressed in this book are solely those of the author. While the accuracy of the facts, as reported by the author, has been verified to the fullest extent possible, the publisher is not liable in any way for the content.

ISBN: 978-81-993018-1-8

Edited by Dipali Singh
Cover design by Syed Dilshad Ali
Typeset by Saanvi Graphics, Noida
Printed and bound in India by Manipal Technologies Limited, Manipal

Contents

Dedication		vii
Foreword by T.P. Sreenivasan		ix
Introduction		xiii
1.	Inspired by a Dream	1
2.	Channeling Inventors' Qualities into Action	11
3.	What Makes an Invention Meaningful?	24
4.	Protecting Your Invention	52
5.	Building the Foundation of a Young Inventor	67
6.	Attitude: Geared to Invention	89
7.	Capitalizing on Your Idea Through Entrepreneurship	126
8.	The Entrepreneur	153
9.	The Intrapreneur	185
10.	Disruptive Innovation	199
11.	The Future of Artificial Intelligence	224

12. Starting Your Own Business	236
13. Rags to Riches: Entrepreneurial Stories	245
14. The Journey of Innovation: Your Turn to Invent and Build the Future	272
About the Author	277

Dedication

I extend my heartfelt gratitude to my family for being an integral part of this journey.

To my wife, Mary—your unwavering support, thoughtful suggestions, kind words, and boundless patience have been a constant source of inspiration throughout this project.

To my daughters, Charlene, and Crystal, and my sons-in-law, Stephen and Nicholas—thank you for your encouragement, motivation, and invaluable assistance along the way.

To my beloved grandchildren, Luke, Lena, Keaton, and Daisy—your love and admiration have filled my heart and strengthened my resolve. You are, and always will be, my greatest cheerleaders.

To my late parents, Paul and Treesa, thank you for instilling in me strong values, a sense of purpose, and the foundation upon which my life has been built.

To my siblings—Joseph, Agnus, Job, Jacob, Elsie, Annie, and Cleetus (of cherished memory), and Mary, James, and Augustine—thank you for your encouragement, belief in my journey, and for sharing in the pride of my accomplishments.

With immense love and gratitude, I dedicate this book to my entire family.

Foreword

Invention, innovation, patents, and Nobel Prizes are often attributed to scientific discoveries that change human life or alter beliefs and theories, which were held sacrosanct for years. With the advent of the internet and now artificial intelligence, changes come faster and dazzling discoveries create disruptive technologies in every sphere of life. But we do not think of thousands of inventions and discoveries through generations which make our lives easier. We take them for granted, such as when we use convenient bags to carry our purchases or use plastic bubbles to pack expensive, but fragile materials.

Charles Kannankeril, who has already obtained 86 patents globally and awaiting 10 more, is no less than those who have transformed human life by working on spectacular technology and products. At a very early age, he learnt the value of timely problem-solving by aiming at customer-focused innovation. Behind the patents that have made errands for ordinary people as unproblematic as possible, there is as much dedication, hard work, ingenuity, and investment.

In his first book, *The Inventor in You* (2018) and in this new one, Charles has not only spelt out the intricacies of the process of inventions but also provided guidelines to capitalize on novel ideas and indicated pathways to popularize and introduce them through industry. Both his books belong to a new genre of writing, highlighting how small inventions and interventions inspire new, young inventors to conceive ideas, implement them, and to change the way of life of new generations.

Charles is among those who not only revolutionizes the lives of ordinary people but also ignites young minds by mentoring them. Though trade secrets have to be respected at every stage, his writings inspire countless young men and women who carry within them a quiet spark, a restlessness to build something of their own, to stand a little taller than their circumstances, and to leave a mark that is unmistakably theirs. Not all of them recognize this and even fewer learn how to nurture it. What distinguishes those who do, is not privilege or luck, but the clarity to listen to that inner call and the discipline to act on it.

This book wakes up that spark. It does not promise shortcuts or miracles. Instead, it offers something far more valuable: a way of thinking and of approaching one's own potential with honesty and courage. The journey of an entrepreneur is not merely about starting a business. It is about building character, resilience, and initiative—qualities that matter just as much in public life as they do in the marketplace.

As someone who spent decades in diplomacy, I have seen how nations rise on the strength of individuals who choose to imagine more for themselves. Innovation, enterprise, and leadership are not abstract ideals. They are lived qualities, revealed in the choices we make each day. The stories and insights in this volume remind us that entrepreneurship is ultimately a human endeavor, shaped by vision, purpose, and an unwavering belief in possibility.

I commend Charles for crafting a work that is both practical and inspiring. It invites readers not only to admire success from afar, but also to discover the entrepreneur within quietly, steadily, and with conviction. The new generation of inventors and entrepreneurs owe a deep debt of gratitude to Charles, not only for inventing little things that have enriched our lives, but also for sharing his secret of success to empower new generations.

I wish the author and the book every success even as he develops his latest interest in playing pickle ball in his spare time.

T.P. Sreenivasan
Former Ambassador of India and Governor for India
at the International Atomic Energy Agency

Introduction

In 2018, shortly after my retirement from a fulfilling 44-year career in innovation, I published my first book, *The Inventor in You*. That book told the story of my journey from a humble village in India to becoming a successful inventor in the US. Growing up with limited resources, I learned early on to make do with what was available. Rather than complaining about what I didn't have, I focused on improvising, adapting, and building solutions from my surroundings. This mindset—rooted in resourcefulness, curiosity, and determination—became the cornerstone of my inventive success.

When I retired, I felt a strong desire to share my experiences and encourage others to explore their own creative potential. I wanted aspiring inventors to know that invention is not the domain of a privileged few—it is an opportunity available to anyone willing to observe, imagine, and act.

Following the publication of my first book, I went on a tour to introduce it and was deeply encouraged by the enthusiasm of readers. Their questions, engagement, and eagerness to learn more were gratifying. What truly moved me, however, was learning that three readers used the techniques from the book to develop their own inventions. That was a profound moment of validation—and true job satisfaction.

I began contemplating on how to continue helping readers on their innovation journeys. But I wasn't sure how to take the next step—until an unusual dream provided unexpected clarity. In the dream, a robot was taking over my life. It was unsettling, even frightening. But upon reflection, I saw it as a metaphor, a reminder of the ever-expanding world of possibilities, and a challenge to reach for greater heights. It forced me to confront a deeper question—not just how to invent, but how to make the most of an invention.

That dream became the spark that inspired this new book.

In *The Inventor in You*, I focused on how to identify problems, develop solutions through invention, and protect those ideas. But inventing something is only the beginning. What happens next—what you do with that idea—is a whole new journey. And that's the purpose of this book: to guide you through the next level.

A great idea, no matter how promising, remains dormant unless acted upon. Without action, it becomes a missed opportunity. This is where entrepreneurial effort becomes essential because:

Innovation without execution is imagination.
Execution without entrepreneurship is limitation.
But innovation with entrepreneurship? That's transformation.

Entrepreneurship is the catalyst that moves an invention from a concept to commercialization. It involves applying strategic thinking, validating market needs, protecting intellectual property, and delivering value—often in the face of uncertainty and resistance. Without this drive, even the most groundbreaking invention can fade into obscurity.

This book focuses on helping inventors and creators to capitalize

> Entrepreneurship is the catalyst that moves an invention from a concept to commercialization.

on their ideas, inventions, and innovations. It explores practical and strategic pathways, including selling or licensing intellectual property, joining a company as an intrapreneur, or launching a new venture as an entrepreneur.

Entrepreneurs and intrapreneurs play a critical role in advancing innovation. They are the ones who dare to challenge convention, disrupt industries, and build something from nothing. Their courage, adaptability, and vision demonstrate that even the simplest ideas can shape industries, improve communities, and change lives.

Invention is not reserved for laboratories or lone geniuses. It is a mindset—available to anyone who approaches the world with curiosity, identifies meaningful problems, and persists through trial and error. Whether you are a student experimenting with a prototype, a professional refining a product, or a retiree dreaming up new possibilities, the spirit of invention is within you.

My own journey—from childhood experiments to decades of innovation and collaboration—has taught me that creativity thrives in environments where exploration is encouraged, failure is embraced as a learning tool, and invention is pursued not just for profit, but for purpose.

The tools, knowledge, and inspiration are within your reach. Whether your contribution is a product, process, solution, or story—it matters. The next big innovation may not come from a major corporation or elite research lab. It might start at your kitchen table, in your garage, or as a fleeting idea that you choose to pursue.

This book is your invitation—to be bold, to think differently, and to believe in the power of your ideas. Within these pages, you'll find the mindset, the methods, and the momentum. But only *you* can take the next step.

Your invention—your vision—can become the next successful product, service, or business if you're willing to believe in it and build it.

Through clear guidance, practical strategies, and real-world insights, my goal is to empower you not just to invent—but to ensure that your innovations have a lasting impact.

1

Inspired by a Dream

My Dream

I finally completed my robotic design. It had been a long and challenging project, but the end result was exactly what I had envisioned—unique and multifunctional. Not only could this robot clean the house, but I had also programmed it to do laundry and even handle some basic cooking tasks. I was incredibly proud of my creation. When I powered it on for the first time, it worked flawlessly, performing every task I had programmed without a hitch. I was thoroughly impressed by its capabilities.

After testing it for a week, I decided to give the robot a break, as I had to leave for a one-day business trip. Before heading out, I powered it down and left it switched off.

When I returned the next day, something felt...strange. My room had been rearranged, and oddly enough, the TV was on—tuned to CNBC, the financial news channel. That struck me as strange since I rarely watch CNBC, and I was sure I had turned the TV off before leaving. Puzzled, I grabbed the remote and switched the TV off—only for it to turn back on again a moment later. This happened several times. Confused and slightly unnerved, I finally noticed the robot—powered on and pointing its fingers at the TV as if controlling it remotely.

My confusion quickly turned to alarm when I saw that my laptop was also on, displaying my investment portfolio. Even more bizarrely, the mouse was moving on its own, executing trades using my retirement fund based on information from CNBC. I turned to see the robot again, this time pointing at the laptop and clearly in control.

I panicked and bolted across the room to shut the robot down. But in my rush, I tripped over a piece of furniture and crashed to the floor, screaming.

That's when I woke up.

It was all just a dream. I'm not a robotics engineer—and there was never a robot in my house to begin with.

Revisiting the Dream of the Thinking Robot

A vivid and unsettling dream, it was one that initially evoked fear but ultimately offered clarity and inspiration. Rather than dismissing it, I found meaning in the experience. The dream served as a powerful metaphor, revealing the vast realm of possibilities in invention and innovation. It challenged me to think not only about how to invent, but how to fully realize the potential of an invention.

In the dream, a robot was gradually taking over my life—an image both disturbing and thought-provoking. Upon reflection, I recognized it as a symbol of the rapidly evolving technological world and the importance of remaining engaged, creative, and forward-thinking. It pushed me to explore new dimensions of innovation and to consider how best to guide others on their own inventive paths.

This dream became the catalyst for writing a new book. It inspired me to share my insights more broadly, with the hope that others may find encouragement, direction, and practical value in their own innovation journeys.

As I reflect on my dream, I realize we may already be laying the groundwork for a future where robots can think independently. Many technologies that once seemed like science fiction—often depicted in movies like James Bond's 007 series—have since become part of our everyday lives. What was once fantasy is now reality, thanks to relentless advances in science and technology.

Given this momentum, it's not far-fetched to believe that some of today's dreams will become tomorrow's realities. We may very well experience the kind of futuristic world I envisioned in my dream. The pace at which technology is evolving suggests that day may come sooner than we expect.

In my research, I came across this statement: *"Artificial Intelligence (AI) plays a crucial role in enabling advanced robotic capabilities, allowing robots to perceive their environment, make decisions, learn from experience, and perform complex tasks that would otherwise require human intervention."* It's evident that AI is the driving force behind intelligent machines, and it's only a matter of time before robots begin thinking in ways that closely resemble human thought.

Could this lead to the emergence of a new robotic race—equal or even superior to humans? If so, it will undoubtedly reshape how we live and think. While that stage may still be at a distance, we are already seeing incredible strides in robotic technology, making our lives easier, more efficient, and more connected.

Invention: The Gateway, Not the Destination

One thing I've learned is that invention is not a dead-end—it's a gateway that opens up a world of possibilities. A single invention can evolve, expand, and create entirely new innovations. With the right mindset and approach, an idea can be optimized and taken to incredible heights, reshaping how we live.

It was this realization, sparked by my dream, that inspired me to write this book.

> A single invention can evolve, expand, and create entirely new innovations.

We live in a fast-moving, tech-driven world where today's innovations can quickly become obsolete. This rapid evolution is fueled by our constant craving for faster, better, and more efficient solutions. That hunger creates an incredible opportunity for creative minds to step up, innovate, and meet the growing demand.

The Inventor in You

As I emphasized in my first book, *The Inventor in You*, everyone has the potential to invent. It starts by proactively identifying problems or unmet needs—then working to solve them with something new, useful, and unique. Inventions don't always have to be revolutionary; sometimes the smallest improvements can make life better, easier, or safer.

The world is full of untapped ideas, products, and processes just waiting to be invented. The opportunities are endless—but so is the competition. Inventors across all fields are racing to be first, and even a brief lapse in attention can mean falling behind. Whether you're developing high-tech systems or improving household tools, staying alert and agile is crucial.

When you have a new idea, be your own toughest critic. Don't just fall in love with your concept—test it. Ask the hard questions: Is it patentable? Is it unique? Is something missing? Is it user-friendly? Can it be made affordably? Will consumers like it? Could it be improved or expanded?

The most successful inventors prioritize solving problems for others—not satisfying their own ego. Your invention must meet real needs, not just impress you or others.

Creativity is the First Step

Creativity begins with the simple act of questioning the status quo. I encourage everyone to develop the habit of recognizing problems and imagining better solutions. That's how inventors are made. Many people hesitate to think of themselves as inventors, imagining that inventors are geniuses or superhumans. But in reality, most inventors are everyday people who simply think differently.

It's all about mindset in how we see the world, how we respond to frustration, and whether we choose to accept things as they are—or challenge them.

I believe there's an inventor in all of us. You may have already taken your first step and not even realized it. Every time you think, *"I've got a great idea,"* or when you get frustrated and say, *"There has to be a better way,"* you're entering the invention process.

You don't need to be a scientist, scholar, or genius to invent something meaningful. In fact, many successful inventions have come from ordinary people with no special training—including children.

Real-life Inspiration: Invention Has No Age

One inspiring example is Dr John Goodenough, who invented the lithium-ion battery at the age of 94. On the other end of the age spectrum, six-year-old Robert Patch created the first toy truck, which became a big hit in the toy industry.

But one of my favorite stories is that of eight-year-old Kylie Simonds, a young cancer patient undergoing chemotherapy. She was tethered to IV bags that hung from a stand, which made it difficult and uncomfortable to move around. One day, while trying to walk, she tripped over a loose tube and fell. Frustrated and hurt, she said to herself, *"There must be a better way to do this."*

As she looked at the IV stand and noticed her backpack nearby, inspiration struck. She asked a nurse if the IV bags could be attached to her backpack. The nurse agreed. Kylie folded the tubes inside the bag, put on the backpack, and walked easily—hands-free and no longer pushing the IV stand.

This small change made a huge difference. She could now move with ease—even climb stairs—while still receiving her treatment. Her parents helped her apply for a US patent for what she named the "IV Pack". At just 10 years of age, Kylie became a patented inventor.

Her story shows that invention doesn't require advanced education or experience—just common sense, creativity, and a strong desire to solve a problem. That's all it takes.

The Inventor's Mindset

Imagine a world without modern transportation, instant communication, or advanced healthcare. It's hard to fathom, yet not so long ago, this was our reality. Thanks to inventors who dared to improve these essential areas, our lives today are vastly more comfortable and connected.

If humanity had been content with what it had, there would have been no progress. We'd still be living in a world with limited tools and minimal convenience. But innovation never rests. In today's fast-paced world, new inventions emerge every day. About 50 years from now, people may look back and wonder how we ever lived without technologies that haven't even been created yet—perhaps, eventually, by *you*.

A Time of Great Opportunity

We're living in one of the most exciting eras for invention. Technology is advancing rapidly, and the demand for faster, smarter, and better tools is insatiable. Devices we consider state-of-the-art today become obsolete within months. This constant cycle of change presents a huge opportunity for creative minds to step forward.

However, opportunity comes with competition. With over 7.5 billion people in the world, it's very likely that someone else has had a similar idea. Patent law in the US grants rights to the *first to file*, not necessarily the first to invent. That means someone else can claim your idea simply by filing before you. Still, this isn't always a problem. If you've come up with the same idea, you might also be the one who improves it, evolves it, or makes it practical.

Many people have great ideas but never act on them. If someone else beat you to filing a patent but never pursued development, there might still be room for your version. We'll discuss patents and intellectual property rights more deeply in a later chapter.

The Nature of Invention

Most inventions are born from effort and determination—not from sudden flashes of brilliance. They arise when you're solving a problem, improving a process, or trying to do something in a better way. Some inventions are even accidents—unexpected results, failed tests, or mistakes that revealed something new.

Often, it's a personal need or frustration that sparks invention. Inventors are naturally curious. They see things differently and ask questions others ignore. They want better answers and are not afraid to step outside the box or challenge conventional thinking.

As young inventor M. Tenith Adithyaa once said: "*I do not want to live with problems; I want to solve them.*" That spirit—combined with ambition, imagination, motivation, inspiration, and persistence—is the essence of an inventor's mindset.

Every time you say, "*There must be a better way,*" you're halfway to inventing something. You already know what's missing. Most people stop there, thinking, "*I'm not an inventor*," or "*What if people laugh at my idea?*" That self-doubt stops countless inventions in their tracks.

But you *are* in a great position. You've used the item, you understand its flaws, and you have insights that even experts might not have. When confidence meets creativity, surprising things can happen.

Specialist vs. Explorer

Some inventors stay within a specific field and become specialists. Others explore broadly, inventing across different areas. The latter may create more diverse but less specialized inventions—think of it like general practitioners versus medical specialists. Personally, I've always leaned toward the explorer mindset. It opens up more opportunities and keeps the work exciting.

For beginners, being an explorer can be especially helpful. You can experiment in areas you already understand, like daily-use items, instead of jumping straight into complex fields like aerospace—unless that's your passion, of course. Start where you're comfortable and grow from there.

Persistence and Accidental Genius

Innovation demands time, effort, and the willingness to fail. Invention doesn't always come from research—it sometimes comes from surprise.

Take the popsicle, for example. Eleven-year-old Frank Epperson mixed soda powder and water with a stick on his porch, then forgot it overnight. By morning, it had frozen around the stick. That happy accident became a cold treat we still enjoy today.

Unexpected results—good or bad—can lead to breakthroughs. Many famous inventions started out as "failures". True inventors don't get discouraged by setbacks—they become curious. They analyze what went wrong and ask what can be learned. Some of history's most useful discoveries began as disappointing experiments.

The Role of Age

You don't need to be a genius, a scientist, or even an adult to invent. Consider five-year-old Sam Houghton, who watched his dad struggle with two types of rakes. Sam tied them together, making a single tool that could handle both jobs. He became the youngest patent holder for his "Improved Broom".

At the other end of the age spectrum, 94-year-old Dr John Goodenough invented a new kind of battery—lightweight, affordable, and potentially transformative for electric cars. As mentioned earlier, he was also one of the co-inventors of the lithium-ion battery, which powers countless devices today.

Invention has no age limit. Whether you're five or 95, what matters is your mindset.

Where Inventions Begin

Inventing starts with curiosity, imagination, and a desire to improve the world around you. Whether you're addressing a need, solving a problem, or simply pursuing a better version of something, your idea can lead to a creation that is extraordinary.

When you get an idea, it's natural to feel excited. You might share it with family and friends. You might even imagine patenting it and becoming financially successful. But before that, always check to see if someone else has already filed for a similar patent. You can do this by using patent databases or even Google.

If you find that your idea has already been patented, don't be discouraged. Look closely—can you improve on it? Many new inventions begin as improvements to existing ones. If you independently created an idea that already exists, that alone shows you're thinking like an inventor. You're in the right league.

Overcoming Disappointment

It can be disheartening to discover that someone else beat you to your idea. But remember, your effort wasn't wasted. Every failure, every roadblock is a step toward developing your inventive skills. Don't let disappointments stop you. Instead, use them to learn and grow.

Invention isn't easy. It takes time, resilience, and hard work. You'll face setbacks. But within every failure is a clue—a valuable one that can guide you to your next idea, your next attempt. Think creatively. Think differently. Think positively.

You're never too young or too old to start inventing.

In the Words of a Legend

I'll end this chapter with a few words from one of the greatest inventors of all time, Thomas Edison:

- *"Genius is one percent inspiration and ninety-nine percent perspiration."*
- *"Opportunity is missed by most people because it is dressed in overalls and looks like work."*

Let these words guide you. Stay curious, work hard, and believe in your ability to create something new. The world needs your ideas.

2

Channeling Inventors' Qualities into Action

If you take a closer look at most inventors, you'll notice they often share five key traits: *ambition, imagination, motivation, inspiration*, and *persistence*. These qualities are the driving force behind their creative breakthroughs and world-changing inventions.

Every great invention begins with a spark—an idea, a question, or even in frustration with the way things are. But ideas alone are not enough. What separates successful inventors from dreamers is not luck or genius, but the deliberate cultivation of qualities that turn thoughts into action. Five qualities mentioned above—ambition, imagination, motivation, inspiration, and persistence—form the bedrock of inventive problem-solving. They are not abstract ideals but practical tools that anyone can learn to apply in their own creative journey.

> If you take a closer look at most inventors, you'll notice they often share five key traits: *ambition, imagination, motivation, inspiration*, and *persistence*.

This chapter explores how to channel these qualities into action, illustrated with stories of inventors past and present, and concludes with practical strategies and exercises you can use to generate ideas and develop solutions to problems you encounter in your own life.

Ambition: Defining the Challenge

Inventors are driven by a powerful ambition—to create something new, useful, and unique. Ambition is more than just a wish; it's a strong inner desire and determination to improve the world through innovation.

While many people have ambition, not everyone acts on it. Some are content with the status quo, satisfied with life as it is. But if everyone had remained that way throughout history, we wouldn't have moved beyond the Stone Age. Ambition fuels progress, and inventors are brimming with it. They set high goals—sometimes even surpassing them—and work tirelessly to achieve them.

But ambition alone isn't enough. The question is: how many of us actually pursue our ambitions with relentless effort?

Often, it takes a personal experience to ignite ambition. Without it, there's no real drive to change. Inventors, however, refuse to accept things as they are. They challenge the status quo.

Take Kylie Simonds, for example. After going through cancer treatment, she was inspired to make life easier for children undergoing chemotherapy. Her ambition led her to invent the pediatric IV backpack—a wearable, kid-friendly IV machine that allows children more freedom during treatment. In 2014, Kylie won an award at the Connecticut Invention Convention and later secured a patent. Her journey shows how ambition can turn a personal challenge into a powerful invention.

Ambition is often misunderstood as mere desire for success or recognition. For inventors, ambition is something deeper—it is the refusal to accept the world as it is and the determination to make it better.

Thomas Edison's ambition to light every home transformed electricity from an experimental curiosity into a universal utility. He saw beyond gas lamps and candles, envisioning a safer, brighter, and more efficient future.

Modern examples of ambition are equally striking. Elon Musk's drive to make humanity a "multiplanetary species" has redefined aerospace engineering. His ambition did not stop at building reusable rockets; it extended to creating a future where space travel is accessible, sustainable, and central to human survival.

How to Apply Ambition Personally

- Ask: "*What problem frustrates me the most?*"
- Define your challenge in terms of impact: "*If I solved this, who would benefit?*"
- Set a goal that feels slightly out of reach.

Ambition is the spark that ensures your work addresses problems worth solving.

Imagination: Envisioning Possibilities

Imagination isn't just a spark—it's the engine of invention. It allows us to venture into uncharted territories, asking bold questions like, "*Why not?*" and imagining possibilities others can't see.

To imagine is to form a mental image of something not currently present or never before seen. It enables inventors to view the ordinary from a new perspective and see potential where others see limitations.

Take this playful example: What's half of the number "eight"? The obvious answer is the number "four". But if you let your imagination explore, you might see an "O" (if you slice it horizontally), or a "three", or even a "W" or "M" (if you slice vertically and rotate the halves). This simple exercise shows how imagination reveals unexpected outcomes by shifting your perspective.

Another example is the evolution of the cell phone. When it first emerged, it was simply a tool to make phone calls, by using a remote. Today, that function represents less than 10 percent of what a smartphone does. Now, we use it to browse the internet, send messages, take photos, stream music and videos, shop, navigate with a Global Positioning System (GPS), and more. Had someone described this vision when mobile phones first came out, they'd have been called a dream. But that's exactly what inventors do—they dream beyond the obvious.

Becky Schroeder, at just 10 years old, imagined a way to do her homework in the dark. Her idea led to the invention of the first glow-in-the-dark writing surface, using phosphorescent paint. In 1974, she became one of the youngest girls to receive a US patent. Her story reminds us that imagination, no matter how small the motivation, can lead to real innovation.

As Albert Einstein once said:

- *"Imagination is more important than knowledge. For knowledge is limited, whereas imagination embraces the entire world."*
- *"Logic will get you from A to B. Imagination will take you everywhere."*

If ambition sets the destination, imagination maps the possibilities. It is the capacity to envision solutions beyond what currently exists.

The Wright brothers were bicycle mechanics, not trained engineers. Yet their imagination enabled them to picture machines that could carry people through the air. Their creative leap—thinking of flight as a matter of balance and control, not just power—allowed them to succeed where others failed.

Today, imagination drives breakthroughs in fields like AI. Developers of generative AI systems imagined machines that could not only process data but also create art, music, and text. What once seemed like science fiction is now shaping industries from healthcare to entertainment.

How to Apply Imagination Personally

- Use "what if" questions to break assumptions.
- Visualize your solution in action, even before you know how to build it.
- Combine unrelated ideas—cross-pollination is vital for originality.

Imagination expands the horizon of what is possible, turning ambition into tangible concepts.

Motivation: Turning Ideas into Action

Motivation—the eagerness to act—is another essential trait of successful inventors. While many people have good ideas, very few take the steps needed to bring them to life.

Too often, we stop at the idea stage. Doubts creep in: *"What if it doesn't work? I don't have the skills. I don't know where to start."* These negative thoughts can kill an idea before it even gets off the ground.

Years later, we may regret not acting—especially when we see someone else turn a similar idea into a successful product. Inventors don't let fear stop them. They are naturally motivated problem-solvers who refuse to live with problematic situations—they fix them.

Take Blaise Pascal. At just 19, he saw how difficult his father's tax calculations were and decided to help. He created a wooden box with dials that could perform quick addition and subtraction.

His invention laid the foundation for the modern calculator—all sparked by the motivation to make his father's work easier.

Having the desire isn't enough. You need the motivation to take that idea and run with it.

Ambition and imagination are powerful, but without motivation they remain dormant. Motivation is the force that moves inventors from thought to action.

Josephine Cochrane's story illustrates this aspect well. Frustrated by the constant chipping of her fine china during handwashing, she resolved to create a better way of cleaning. Her personal motivation led to the invention of the modern dishwasher, which transformed domestic life worldwide.

On a global scale, innovators working on renewable energy are motivated by the urgent challenge of climate change. From solar power advances to wind turbine design, motivation to address a pressing problem has brought in a wave of new technologies reshaping how the world produces energy.

How to apply motivation personally

- Identify your personal stake: *"Why does this problem matter to me?"*
- Break large goals into small, achievable steps.
- Build accountability by sharing your progress with others.

Motivation ensures that ideas do not remain theoretical but move steadily toward reality.

Inspiration: Discovering Sparks in the World Around You

Inspiration is the light that ignites creativity. It's the mental stimulation that pushes inventors to imagine new possibilities and then act on them.

Inventors are often inspired by stories, challenges, or personal experiences. They relate to others who've succeeded and channel that energy into their own work. Inspiration helps connect the dots between what is and what could be.

Remya Jose, a 14-year-old from Kerala, India, created a pedal-powered washing machine when her family couldn't afford electricity. Using an old bicycle and a tub, she built an eco-friendly machine that washed clothes and promoted exercise—all without power. Her ability to combine creativity and practicality is what made her invention stand out.

Inspiration encourages inventors to ask: *What else is possible?* And from there, they build on the solution.

While motivation drives action, inspiration provides fresh insight. It often arises from close observation, nature, or unexpected experiences.

George de Mestral's invention of "velcro" is a classic case. After a walk in the woods, he noticed burrs clinging stubbornly to his dog's fur. Instead of dismissing it, he studied them under a microscope and discovered their hooklike structure. This simple moment of observation became the basis for a fastening system now used everywhere from sneakers to space suits.

Modern inspiration often comes from unexpected intersections. For instance, medical researchers inspired by gecko feet have developed new adhesive bandages that stick without glue, mimicking the natural grip of the reptile's tiny hairs.

How to apply inspiration personally

- Pay attention to frustrations, oddities, and small details.
- Capture first signs of insights in a notebook or phone app.
- Seek ideas outside your own field.

Inspiration sharpens creativity, guiding inventors toward elegant and effective solutions.

Persistence: The Power to Keep Going

Persistence—the determination to venture forward despite difficulties—is often what separates those who dream from those who deliver.

The path to invention is rarely smooth. Most inventors face multiple failures, disappointments, and mishaps. But rather than giving up, they treat each failure as a learning experience.

Thomas Edison is a shining example. He famously said, *"I have not failed. I've just found 10,000 ways that won't work."* Edison's perspective turned every setback into a stepping stone, leading to one of the most prolific careers in invention history.

Persistence is about pushing through even when the outcome is uncertain. It's about refusing to give up.

Peter Chilvers, at 12, was bored with traditional surfing and sought something more exciting. After countless failed attempts to modify his board, he didn't give up. Eventually, he added a sail—and in 1958, created the world's first sailboard.

Persistence means staying committed to a vision, even when the road is long.

Perhaps the most vital quality of all is persistence. Ambition, imagination, motivation, and inspiration all play roles in sparking ideas, but persistence ensures they reach completion.

James Dyson exemplifies this quality. He built more than 5,000 prototypes before creating his successful bagless vacuum cleaner. Each failed attempt was not a defeat but a step closer to success. His persistence turned frustration into one of the most successful household innovations of the modern era.

Even in cutting-edge fields like AI, persistence is the force behind progress. Breakthroughs often come only after years of trial, error, and refinement. Self-driving car technology, for example, has taken decades of persistent development, with countless failures and iterations, to approach its reliable operation.

How to apply persistence personally

- Expect setbacks—they are part of the process.
- Document your progress and learn from mistakes.
- Reframe failure as a welcome feedback.

Persistence is the quality that transforms determination into achievement.

Putting it All Together: From Qualities to Solutions

Each of these five qualities—*ambition, imagination, motivation, inspiration, and persistence*—is powerful on its own. But together, they form the foundation of every great invention. Without even one, the journey becomes harder, and the destination may remain out of reach.

Together, they form a cycle of invention:

1. *Ambition* defines the challenge.
2. *Imagination* envisions possibilities.
3. *Motivation* propels action.
4. *Inspiration* refines the approach.
5. *Persistence* carries the idea through obstacles.

This cycle applies not only to life-changing inventions but also to everyday problem-solving. Whether developing clean-energy technologies, designing an easier way to carry groceries, or creating a tool to save time at work, these five qualities provide the mindset and method to turn problems into solutions.

Conclusion: The Inventor's Mindset

History's greatest inventors were not born extraordinary; they became extraordinary by cultivating qualities that anyone can develop. Edison, the Wright brothers, Josephine Cochrane, George de Mestral, James Dyson, Elon Musk, and countless others show us that invention is a human endeavor, built on determination and vision.

The world today faces enormous challenges—climate change, resource scarcity, healthcare demands, and technological disruption. Each of these challenges is also an opportunity for invention. By pursuing your ambition, imagination, motivation, inspiration, and persistence, you too can contribute solutions, whether in small personal ways or through ideas that ripple across industries.

The future is not written by chance; it is shaped by those willing to act. The question is: how will you channel your qualities to invent, to solve, and to create?

Inventor's Qualities Workbook

Use this worksheet to practice focusing on your ambition, imagination, motivation, inspiration, and persistence. Fill it out as you work through a problem or idea.

Ambition: Defining the Challenge

Exercises and Notes

1. List three problems that frustrate you daily.
    i. ....
    ii. ....
    iii. ....

2. Circle the one problem with the biggest impact if solved.

   i. Problem Chosen: ....

3. Write your challenge as a goal statement.

   i. "I want to improve .... by .... "

☐ Did I choose a challenge that excites me?

Imagination: Envisioning Possibilities

1. Brainstorm 10 wild or unconventional solutions to your chosen problem.

   i. ....   vi. ....
   ii. ....   vii. ....
   iii. ....   viii. ....
   iv. ....   ix. ....
   v. ....   x. ....

2. Highlight two solutions worth exploring further.

   i. Idea #1: ....

   ii. Idea #2: ....

   Sketch or outline these solutions.   [Space for drawings/notes]

☐ Did I push past "obvious" ideas and stretch my thinking?

Motivation: Turning Ideas into Action

1. Write why solving this problem matters to you.
   i. ....

2. Break your idea into three small steps you can do this week.

   Step 1:...

   Step 2:...

   Step 3:...

3. Identify someone to share your progress with.
   Accountability Partner: ....

☐ Do I feel personally invested in this solution?

Inspiration: Discovering Sparks Around You

1. Observe your surroundings and list five interesting or odd things. (For example, how a leaf sheds water, how a tool is used differently than intended.)

   i. ....

   ii. ....

   iii. ....

   iv. ....

   v. ....

2. Ask: Could any of these apply to my problem?

   Possible connections: ....

3. Record new ideas inspired by these observations.

   i. ....

   ii. ....

☐ Did I stay curious and open-minded today?

Persistence: The Power to Keep Going

1. Commit to working on your idea for 15 minutes daily for seven days.

    Start Date: .... End Date: ....

2. Daily log – What worked, what failed, what I learned.

    Day 1: ....

    Day 2: ....

    Day 3: ....

    Day 4: ....

    Day 5: ....

    Day 6: ....

    Day 7: ....

3. Review at the end of the week.

    Key Insights: ....

☐ Did I make steady progress, even when it was difficult?

✓ Reflection Box

   What did I learn about myself through this exercise?

   ....

   ....

   ....

   ....

   ....

   ....

3

What Makes an Invention Meaningful?

The Foundation of Great Inventions

To create a successful invention, one must first understand what qualifies as a meaningful and impactful innovation. While people create inventions with varying levels of significance, the most valuable ones solve real problems or fulfill unmet needs. These inventions tend to be marketable and can generate substantial financial rewards.

The process starts with listening to consumers and being willing to question the status quo. A successful invention often emerges from a desire to do something differently—and better. Once you've formed your idea, don't stop at celebration. Be your own toughest critic. Examine your invention for flaws, market limitations, or potential consumer resistance. Ask yourself: *"Does this invention truly solve the problem it's intended to address?"*

A good inventor maintains an open mind, focuses on practical solutions, and resists the temptation to be driven by ego. The goal is not just to invent something for its own sake, but to create value by solving real problems.

From Idea to Impact: A Four-step Process

Creating a valuable invention involves four key stages:

1. *Start with the Right Idea*
   Identify a problem worth solving or a need worth fulfilling.
2. *Develop a Functional Invention*
   Transform your idea into a creation that actually works.
3. *Protect it with a Patent Strategy*
   Understand the legal process and safeguard your invention.
4. *Explore the Market*
   Find the audience, refine the message, and scale your impact.

Sometimes, growth comes not from a new invention, but from improving or adapting an existing one. Expansion can mean new features, markets, or entirely different applications.

What is an Invention?

Before diving into how to invent, let's define what an invention actually is.

Official Definitions

- *An invention is the creation of something entirely new through individual ideas and development.*
- The US Patent and Trademark Office (USPTO) defines an invention as any *process, machine, manufacture,* or *composition of matter*, or any useful *improvement* thereof.
- In patent terms, an invention must have *a technical character*, solve a *technical problem*, and include *technical features*.

To qualify for a *utility patent* in the US, your invention must meet four essential criteria:

1. *Patentable Subject Matter*

   It must be technical—not abstract concepts or natural phenomena.

2. *Novelty*

   It must be new and not previously disclosed.

3. *Utility*

   It must serve a practical purpose.

4. *Non-obviousness*

   It must be inventive—not something easily deduced by others in the field.

To illustrate these criteria, consider a hypothetical scenario involving two teams working on bicycle helmets:

- *Team A* repaints the helmet in a bright color to improve its appearance.
- *Team B* redesigns the helmet to make it foldable, solving the issue of portability.

Now let's evaluate:

- *Patentable Subject Matter*: Painting a helmet doesn't qualify; redesigning it does.
- *Novelty*: A new color isn't novel; a foldable design is.
- *Utility*: A new paint job lacks purpose; a compact design improves functionality.
- *Non-obviousness*: Painting is obvious; folding requires creative development.

Only *Team B* meets all four criteria and qualifies for patent protection.

Types of Inventions

Inventions generally fall into two broad categories:

1. *Original Inventions*

    These are entirely new concepts, such as the light bulb, automobile, airplane, or steam engine. They form the foundation for countless future innovations.

2. *Improvements and Modifications*

    Most modern inventions build on existing concepts. They are upgrades, extensions, or new versions of older ideas. This makes them more achievable for most inventors—and often just as valuable.

    Such derivative inventions are often easier to develop because they build upon existing frameworks. Original inventions, by contrast, begin from a blank slate and require identifying a problem, devising a unique solution, and implementing it through considerable effort and risk.

    Nevertheless, original inventions continue to emerge. Examples from recent decades include the internet, smartphones, GPS, 3D printers, online banking, and advanced robotics.

Case Study: The Chair

The chair began as a simple stool. Over time, it evolved into armchairs, rocking chairs, wheelchairs, baby strollers, folding chairs, and endless reinventions—all based on the original concept. Each version met a new need or solved a unique problem.

Other evolving inventions include:

- *Automobiles* evolved from manually cranked engines to self-driving vehicles.
- *Computers* shrank from room-sized machines (costing millions of dollars) to powerful handheld devices (costing only a few hundreds of dollars).
- *Toothbrushes* diversified into countless designs, each with a specific purpose.

Paradigm Shifts

Original inventions are rarer because they start from a blank slate and involve identifying a new need, crafting a solution, and developing it into a product. Nevertheless, groundbreaking inventions continue to emerge, such as the internet, smartphones, 3D printing, GPS, online banking, and advanced robotics.

Some of these are considered *paradigm shifts*—inventions that have dramatically changed the way people live, work, and communicate. Examples include:

- Printing press
- Telephone
- Antibiotics
- DNA structure discovery
- Nuclear power
- The internet
- The smartphone

These inventions often required years of collaboration and research by multiple inventors and scientists. But not all original inventions are complex. Some simple ideas became massively successful due to clever designs and brilliant marketing, like Lego, the Hula Hoop, and the Pet Rock.

How to Generate Invention Ideas

Opportunities for invention abound across all sectors, from cutting-edge technologies to everyday household items. In today's fast-paced world, where innovations emerge rapidly and obsolescence is common, being proactive and forward-thinking is crucial.

Ideas are the seeds of every invention. But how do you find them? Ideas often arise from unmet needs. If you've ever thought, "*I wish there were a better way to do this,*" you've stumbled upon the starting point for invention.

> Ideas are the seeds of every invention. But how do you find them? Ideas often arise from unmet needs.

Here are four proven strategies to spark invention ideas:

1. Identify an Unmet Need

Most inventions solve problems. Pay attention to what frustrates people. What tasks are harder than they should be?

Focus on everyday problems. Even small inconveniences can lead to huge opportunities. For instance, students struggling to carry books inspired the invention of the *modern backpack*, a product now used by nearly every student worldwide. Today, the global backpack market is worth over $20 billion.

2. Pay Attention to Wishes and Fantasies

What do people *wish* existed?

- "*I wish my dishes cleaned themselves.*"
- "*I wish my dog could talk.*"
- "*I wish my food wouldn't get cold so quickly.*"

These aren't just fantasies—they're clues to future inventions.

3. Anticipate What's Becoming Obsolete

Innovation thrives on improvement. Many common products today are heading toward obsolescence. Every product has a life cycle. What are we using today that won't be around in 10 years?

- Credit cards → digital wallets
- Gas vehicles → electric and autonomous cars
- Manual vacuums → robot vacuums

Spotting these trends early gives you the chance to create the next generation of solutions. Spot the trend. Be the solution.

4. Challenge the Status Quo

Good inventors ask: *"Why are we still doing it this way?"*

Be proactive. Continuously ask: *"How can this be improved?" "What would make it faster, safer, smaller, or more user-friendly?"* This mindset is especially vital in fast-moving fields like AI, robotics, and wearable tech.

Take a closer look at:

- How things are made
- How people interact with products
- How technology could enhance an experience

Improvement is always possible—and invention begins with that belief.

Invention is Within Reach

We live in an era of unprecedented opportunity. As technology advances and society evolves, new needs emerge every day. That means *your* next idea could be the fire that changes the world—or simply makes life a little easier for someone.

Invention isn't reserved for geniuses or scientists. It belongs to the curious, the persistent, and the brave.

Discovering Inventive Opportunities through Observation and Modification

Section 1: Identifying Problems in Everyday Products

Most people view new products through a lens of excitement and convenience, often overlooking flaws or limitations. Over time, as these products are used more frequently, some users begin to notice shortcomings—issues that may cause frustration or dissatisfaction. While many accept these flaws due to a lack of alternatives, a select few see them as opportunities. These individuals question the status quo, seek solutions, and in doing so, often arrive at new inventions.

Opportunities for innovation are everywhere. We use countless tools and appliances daily—many of which fall short of our expectations in one way or another. How often have you found yourself saying, *"I wish this product didn't break so easily,"* or *"It's too slow,"* or *"It's not user-friendly,"* *"It's too loud,"* *"The design is bulky,"* or *"The battery life is too short"*? These everyday inconveniences represent a wealth of untapped potential for improvement and innovation.

Case Study: The Knife

The knife—one of humanity's oldest tools—is both essential and inherently dangerous. Despite its usefulness, the sharp edge poses a safety risk. For generations, this risk was tolerated. Eventually, inventors addressed it by creating folding knives and retractable blades to reduce accidental contact. Others approached the issue differently by inventing cut-resistant gloves, which didn't alter the knife itself but enhanced user safety. These gloves are now mandatory in many industrial settings, demonstrating the effectiveness of this solution.

In fact, a simple online search on "knife safety" will reveal an array of safety devices and gadgets—each representing a thoughtful response to a real-world problem. This pattern illustrates a fundamental principle of invention: by recognizing and solving problems, we make life safer, easier, and more efficient.

It's worth noting that early solutions are often partial or imperfect. Even when an inventor produces a well-received solution, further improvements may soon follow. This ongoing evolution is a natural and vital part of the invention process—one that ensures continued innovation and progress.

This pattern—recognizing a flaw and designing a solution—is foundational to invention. Consider modern tools like solar-powered calculators or cordless vacuums. Each arose from a simple thought: "*There must be a better way.*"

Section 2: Modifying Existing Products to Enhance Functionality

Another inventive path involves modifying an existing product to improve its function or expand its capabilities. Often, people rely on multiple tools to complete a single task, accepting inefficiencies. Inventive minds ask: "*Can these tools be combined or improved?*"

Case Study: The Floor Cleaner Dilemma

Another common approach to invention involves modifying existing products. This typically means altering a product's features, structure, or functionality to either enhance its performance or enable it to serve multiple purposes. These modifications can result in a significantly improved version of the original product or an entirely new multifunctional tool.

For example, consider the process of cleaning a kitchen floor. Traditionally, this task involves three distinct tools: a vacuum cleaner to collect debris, a mop to wash the floor, and a dry mop or towel to remove moisture. Most people accept this laborious process as the norm. However, a creative thinker might ask, "*Why not create a single tool that performs all three functions?*"

Upon inspection, a vacuum cleaner and mop share several physical similarities: both have a long handle, a base that contacts the floor, and a back-and-forth motion during use. This observation opens the door to innovation. One might design a dual-purpose device by attaching a mop sponge to the opposite side of a vacuum's base. The operator could then flip the appliance to switch between vacuuming and mopping. Further enhancements might include a water spray nozzle to wet the floor before mopping.

Taking it a step further, inventive minds might notice that vacuum cleaners expel warm air after filtration. This often-overlooked feature could be repurposed to dry the floor after mopping. By installing a switch to alternate between vacuuming and hot air blowing, the user could create a three-in-one cleaning device: vacuum, mop, and dryer.

This process—recognizing inefficiencies, identifying complementary functionalities, and creatively combining features—is at the heart of many successful inventions.

Real-world examples abound

- Sam Houghton, who became the youngest patent holder at age five, solved a simple problem faced by his father while raking leaves. Observing the inconvenience of switching between two rakes for coarse and fine debris, he tied them together to create a single dual-sided tool—the *Improved Broom*.

- *Screwdrivers* initially came in one shape and size. Over time, multiple sizes and head types emerged, leading to cluttered toolboxes. One inventor addressed this by designing a universal handle that could hold interchangeable screwdriver tips, storing them within the handle itself.
- The *Swiss Army Knife* began as a folding knife and evolved into a multifunctional tool including a screwdriver, can opener, scissors, and more.
- *Bubble Mailers* were developed by laminating an outer film to bubble wrap, creating a cushioned envelope ideal for shipping delicate items.
- The *Salad Spinner* was created by placing a colander inside a spinning bowl with a lid, offering a quick and efficient method to dry washed greens.
- *Make-up Compacts* were enhanced by adding mirrors to the inside of the lid, enabling easier application.
- The *Walking Stick Seat* combines a walking aid and a portable seat—a perfect solution for individuals who need both.
- *Refrigerators* evolved from simple cooling units to include freezers, ice dispensers, digital displays, and recipe suggestions.
- *Alarm Clocks* became multifunctional with the addition of radios, combining music, news, and timekeeping in a single device.

Each of these products began as a single-function tool and was improved through thoughtful, purposeful modification.

Section 3: Discovering New Uses for Familiar Objects

Sometimes, invention doesn't require changing a product—but rather, changing how it's used. This inventive thinking begins with curiosity, a willingness to challenge assumptions, and an openness to new possibilities.

Identifying new applications for an existing product is one of the most accessible and powerful forms of invention. This process begins with questioning the status quo, maintaining curiosity, resisting tunnel vision, and embracing creative thinking.

Most people view products only within the context of their intended use. Inventors, by contrast, look beyond this—asking how a product's features might be leveraged in new or unexpected ways.

A prime example is the *cell phone*. Originally developed as a portable communication device, it has since evolved into an indispensable tool that serves as a camera, GPS navigator, internet browser, gaming device, productivity assistant, banking terminal, and much more. Today, actual voice communication comprises a small fraction of a smartphone's overall use.

Each of these additional functions—messaging, photography, social networking, and app usage—represents a new invention layered onto the original product. This transformative evolution is a hallmark of inventive thinking.

Another compelling example is *Bubble Wrap*. Initially created as a textured wallpaper, it failed in that role. However, its cushioning properties were soon recognized, and it was repurposed as protective packaging. Further applications emerged:

- *Insulation*: The air-filled bubbles provided thermal insulation in various environments.
- *Swimming pool covers*: Bubble wrap retained solar heat and prevented water evaporation.

- *Stress relief:* Psychologists found popping the bubbles helped reduce anxiety.
- *Toys*: Bubble wrap was modified into playful, tactile products in various colors and scents.
- *Reusable ice packs*: Water-filled bubble wrap was frozen to create cold therapy packs.

What began as a failed wall covering transformed into a product with hundreds of uses. In fact, a book titled *A Thousand Uses for Bubble Wrap* was published, showcasing the product's versatility. Many of these adaptations are now patented inventions.

Other examples of repurposing include:

- *Baking soda,* initially developed for baking, is now used for cleaning, deodorizing, toothpaste, and personal care.
- *Duct tape*, originally designed for military use, has found applications in home repair, crafting, and even fashion.
- *Cornstarch* is used not only in cooking but also in biodegradable plastics, baby powder, and medical products.

Section 4: Strategies to Sharpen Your Inventive Mind

To cultivate your own inventive vision:

- *Observe Problems Closely*: What frustrates you or slows you down?
- *Ask Questions*: "Why is this process done this way? Could it be done better?"
- *Challenge Assumptions*: "Must this product only do one thing?"
- *Look Across Fields*: Could an idea from another industry apply here?

- *Keep a Journal*: Record problems, odd ideas, and unusual combinations.

Thinking Like an Inventor

Inventive thinking doesn't always require creating something entirely new. It often begins with the simplest insight: "Something could be better." Often, it involves observing the world more deeply—identifying problems in existing products, finding ways to improve or combine them, or recognizing entirely new applications for them. Whether through addressing product limitations, enhancing functionality, or repurposing items in creative ways, these approaches form the foundation of innovation.

Everything around you—whether it delights or frustrates—holds potential for reinvention. See what others overlook. Question what others accept. Imagine what others don't. In doing so, you'll take the first step toward becoming an inventor

By adopting a mindset that constantly questions, analyzes, and imagines alternatives, anyone can become part of the inventive process. The world is filled with opportunities for improvement—it simply requires the right perspective to see them.

The Invention Process

From Idea to Innovation

Now that you understand how to generate ideas for an invention, let's look at the next stage—the *Invention Process*. I've simplified this journey into three critical steps that guide every successful invention:

Why to Invent, What to Invent, and How to Invent

Each step answers a fundamental question that brings clarity and direction to your creative process.

1. Why Invent?

Invention without purpose is like building a bridge to nowhere. The first step is to *identify the purpose, the reason, or the unmet need.* This step lays the foundation for your invention journey.

Recognizing the Need

Every invention starts with a problem. Think of it as a trigger—something isn't working, or something is missing.

> *Imagine someone driving on a rough road who gets a flat tire and misses an important appointment. Frustrated, the person says, "I wish there was a tire that won't go flat!"* That emotional outburst is a goldmine—it reveals an unmet need. The need for a puncture-proof tire.

As an inventor, your job is to recognize such needs. Problems are everywhere, and each one is an opportunity in disguise.

Observation is Key

Inventors observe the world differently. When something breaks, takes too long, or doesn't work as expected, they don't just complain—they see a chance to improve it.

2. What to Invent?

Once you've identified the problem, it's time to figure out *what* to create that solves it.

Generating Possibilities

Let's go back to our tire example. Possible solutions could include:

- A tougher rubber compound
- A puncture-proof inner core
- Airless tires using foam or spring suspension

But just having ideas isn't enough. At this stage, they're *concepts*, not inventions. You must *evaluate, combine, and refine* them to shape an inventive solution.

Questions to Ask

- "*What is the specific challenge?*"
- "*What existing solutions are inadequate?*"
- "*How can I improve or reimagine this?*"

This step often involves *brainstorming, mind mapping,* or *free association* to spark creativity.

3. How to Invent?

Now comes the real work—*turning your idea into reality.*
Development and Prototyping
You need to:

- Research existing technologies
- Test different materials or configurations
- Choose the most promising option to develop

In some cases, you may explore multiple solutions in parallel. Evaluate them for:

- Technical feasibility
- Cost-effectiveness
- Intellectual property potential

For the tire example, inventors might try laminating the rubber with a metal plate, or replacing air with durable foam.

Eventually, this stage culminates in a working solution—a product, process, or combination of both—that can be developed, tested, refined, and protected. The real labor of invention lies in this development phase, which is often the most demanding and resource-intensive.

The Real Work of Inventing

While the first step—identifying the problem—is crucial, the *real effort* is in the *second and third steps*: generating and developing ideas. These require persistence, creativity, and an analytical mindset.

Identifying Problems: Industry vs. Independent Inventors

Not all inventors are responsible for identifying the problem. In corporate environments, customers, sales representatives, or marketing teams often provide inputs on product issues or unmet needs. Independent inventors, however, typically take full responsibility for problem identification.

To identify problems, stay observant. Watch how people interact with tools and everyday products. Ask questions like: "*What do I like or dislike about this?*" "*How can it be improved?*" These simple observations can yield a multitude of inventive opportunities.

The Inventor's Mindset

Inventors challenge the status quo. When they use a tool or appliance, they don't just use it—they critique it.

"*Is the vacuum cleaner too noisy? Too heavy? Hard to clean?*"

This critical curiosity leads to dozens of *invention ideas*. For example:

- A vacuum with built-in mopping and waxing
- Ergonomic, quieter, lightweight vacuums
- Smart filter replacement alerts

Everyday Inspiration: Simple Actions, Big Ideas

You are surrounded by opportunities to invent. Examine your daily routine—from brushing your teeth to working, shopping, and relaxing. Ask yourself: "*Is there a better, faster, or safer way to do this?*"

Even a basic tool like a screwdriver has evolved over time. From the flat head to the Philips, and eventually to interchangeable multihead designs, each iteration addressed a particular inconvenience. Likewise, new ideas often stem from dissatisfaction with existing solutions.

Wish Lists and Opportunities

Great ideas often begin with:

"*I wish I had...*" or "*I wish I could...*"

Every time someone says that, you've been handed a *potential invention*.

Keep a wish list journal. Record complaints, annoyances, or suggestions—yours or by others'. These are seeds for innovation.

Analyze Your Daily Life

From morning routines to bedtime rituals, every action involves tools, products, or processes.

Ask yourself: "Am I happy with how this works? Can it be better, faster, safer, or easier?"

Think about:

- Kitchen tools
- Transportation
- Cleaning routines
- Work tools
- Leisure and entertainment devices

Improving What Already Exists

Most inventions are *improvements* on what came before.

Take the screwdriver:

- Flathead → Philips → Allen → Interchangeable heads
- Compact handle with snap-on heads → Electric screwdrivers

Ask yourself:

"*What's the next evolution of this tool?*"
Safety as a Catalyst for Invention
A powerful driver of innovation is safety.

Despite existing features, people still get hurt using everyday products. Pay particular attention to safety. Every consumer product has room for safety improvements.

Inventors can add:

- Skid-resistant soles
- Child-proof appliances
- Grills with built-in fire extinguishers

Each unsafe experience is a call to invent something better.

Inventing Within an Industry

If you're employed in an industry, invention opportunities extend beyond product design. In a company, your expertise gives you unique insight into:

- Raw materials
- Manufacturing processes
- Customer feedback
- Competitor weaknesses

Machine operators, engineers, and salespeople have all brought about product and process improvements by simply observing their everyday work.

Research and Development (R&D) professionals often collaborate with sales and marketing to understand customer needs. A deep understanding of competitors' products also helps identify weaknesses that your invention can address. R&D teams may also develop "pet projects", using existing technologies to create entirely new offerings.

Repurposing products is another powerful avenue for invention. Consider how bubble wrap, originally designed for packaging, was later adapted for pool covers, insulated envelopes, and even drainage solutions.

Harnessing the Power of Brainstorming

The most effective brainstorming involves a mix of perspectives—engineers, marketers, users—all contributing ideas without fear of judgment. The goal is quantity over quality in the initial stages, allowing creativity to flow. Sometimes a seemingly silly idea sparks a great one.

In a brainstorming session:

- All ideas are welcome
- No judgment—what sounds trivial may give birth to a brilliant thought
- Ideas build on each other

Whether with a team or alone, *divergent thinking* helps you discover unexpected solutions.

Independent inventors can simulate brainstorming by putting themselves in the roles of various stakeholders. Try to think like a marketer, a customer, or a competitor. This method can generate unique insights that may not arise from a single point of view.

Avoid tunnel vision. Don't focus only on conventional approaches. Think beyond the obvious. For example, addressing the need for quicker floor cleaning might involve combining a vacuum and mop into one machine, streamlining multiple tasks into a single operation.

My Secret Technique: Mental Prototyping

Many inventors use mental rehearsal as a powerful technique. Before engaging in physical development, visualize the process, simulate solutions, and analyze challenges mentally. This practice accelerates problem-solving and enhances creative thinking.

When I work independently, I use this mental visualization technique. It goes like this:

1. Go to a quiet place.
2. Close your eyes.
3. Focus intensely on the challenge.
4. Imagine shapes, materials, and movements.
5. Manipulate and mentally prototype your idea.

Over the years, I've trained myself to do this naturally—even mid-conversation. This state of mental "solitude" has helped me come up with some of my best ideas.

The Invention Process is a Way of Life

The invention process is both an art and a science. It isn't limited to scientists or engineers. It's about how you see the world. Once you train your mind to look for problems, analyze solutions, and imagine improvements, you'll realize that opportunities for invention are *everywhere*.

The process of inventing can be as simple or as complex as the problem demands. But the approach—*why, what,* and *how to invent*—remains constant.

In the next section, we'll look at *simple invention examples* to show how everyday challenges have led to clever, practical solutions.

Opportunities to invent are all around you—waiting to be noticed, explored, and brought to life.

From Brainstorming to Breakthrough

Brainstorming Sessions: Gathering Ideas

Sessions of brainstorming are incredibly useful for collecting a broad range of ideas and solutions. At the end of a productive session, it is likely you'll have several potential paths to follow. However, it's important to remember that not every idea can—or should—be developed. Testing each would be too time-consuming and expensive. You'll need a system to *narrow down your options*.

Screening Ideas: Matching Features

To streamline this process, start by listing all *required features* of your final product in the first column of a Table. Below that, add *value-added features* that aren't essential but would enhance the product. Then, across the top row, list your ideas.

For each idea, mark whether it satisfies each feature. Discard any idea that fails to meet all the required features. Next, prioritize the remaining ideas based on how many value-added features they include.

Table 1: Screening Ideas by Matching Features

Minimum Required Features	Idea #1	Idea #2	Idea #3	Idea #4
A	YES	YES	YES	YES
B	YES	YES	YES	YES
C	NO	YES	YES	YES
D	NO	YES	YES	YES
Additional Features				
E	NO	NO	YES	YES
F	NO	NO	NO	YES

In this example:

- Ideas 2, 3, and 4 meet all *minimum required* features.
- Ideas 3 and 4 also meet *value-added features*—with Idea 4 outperforming all others.
- Idea 4 rises to the top, followed by Idea 3, then Idea 2. Idea 1 is disqualified.

Depending on your resources, you may choose more than one idea for further development. But before finalizing, conduct a *feasibility screening*.

Feasibility Screening: From Concept to Reality

The next stage involves evaluating ideas based on development challenges, cost, regulations, and more.

Table 2: Screening Ideas for Feasibility

Feasibility	Idea #2	Idea #3	Idea #4
Development	GOOD	GOOD	POOR
Manufacturing	GOOD	GOOD	FAIR
Cost	GOOD	GOOD	FAIR
Regulations	GOOD	GOOD	GOOD
Sustainability	GOOD	GOOD	GOOD
Intellectual Property	FAIR	GOOD	GOOD

After this round, Idea 3 becomes the leading option due to development ease and lower cost, despite having fewer features than Idea 4.

Turning Ideas into Products: The Development Stage

Once an idea has passed both screenings, you're ready to enter the most challenging part: *product development.*

Remember: *An idea is not yet an invention.* It becomes an invention only when it is proven and implemented successfully.

To bring an idea to life, you'll need creativity, technical skill, and a lot of perseverance.

Brainstorming Again: For Solutions

In this stage, you'll again brainstorm to identify the best path forward. Multiple solutions may arise, each needing testing, modeling, or prototyping. You must *select a solution* and begin creating a model to validate it.

Methods for Visualizing Product Designs

You can use several methods to visualize or screen your models:

- *Mental Exercise*: Done without tools, this is a fast, flexible method that relies on strong memory and imagination.
- *Sketching*: A traditional pencil-and-paper approach, it is the best for simpler two-dimensional visuals.
- *Computer Modeling*: Provides three-dimensional renderings and is useful for more complex designs.

Personally, I prefer the mental exercise technique. It allows instant reconfiguration of parts and testing of ideas in real time, anywhere—even in the shower!

Prototyping: Building the First Model

The final proof of any invention lies in the prototype. Start simple, using materials like glue, rubber bands, or Plaster of Paris to keep costs low.

I often used items from the Home Depot—like a toilet tank float—to mimic parts in my design.

A prototype should be functional, not perfect. You'll often go through multiple versions before reaching a viable one.

My Braided Paper Prototype

One of my inventions involved a machine that twisted and braided continuous sheets of paper. My prototype included:

- Scrap wood
- Two toilet tank floats
- A $15 handheld electric drill

Despite its simplicity, the prototype performed exceptionally, producing braided paper at *200 feet per minute* for under $25. It gained the attention of top executives, including the CEO, who was amazed by its cost-efficiency and effectiveness.

Case Study: Invention in Action

Let's walk through a real-world example of this entire process.

Step 1: Identifying a Problem

Spectators at sporting events were suffering from sun exposure, heatstroke, and discomfort.

Step 2: Brainstorming Solutions

1. Tell them to go home
2. Give out fans
3. Recommend hats
4. Modify hats for shade
5. Use tinted visors
6. Block the sun with opaque film
7. Add reflective surfaces

8. Add *solar panels + fan*
9. Drink water
10. Use cool cloths

Step 3: Selecting the Best Idea

Idea #8—a hat with *solar panels powering a fan*—was unique and promising. All other ideas are either existing solutions or offer limited innovation.

Before development, conduct a *prior art search* to avoid duplicating existing inventions.

Developing the Product

Start by imagining or sketching the hat with:

- Flexible solar panels on top
- A small fan near the face
- Internal wiring and lightweight battery

Create a *series of prototypes* to test the design. Refine it through trial and error, then move forward with *patent protection.*

Thinking Beyond the First Design

True inventors never stop improving. You may ask:

- Can the fan run on battery when it's cloudy?
- Can we adapt the hat for *construction workers* or *military personnel?*

Hard hats and helmets are actually easier to modify than cloth hats—another potential opportunity!

Final Thoughts

The invention process is not a straight line but a dynamic journey. It involves identifying real-world problems, generating and screening ideas, developing low-cost prototypes, testing solutions, and continually seeking improvements. Successful inventors combine imagination with practicality, and creativity with discipline. Your first invention may only be the beginning of a much larger journey.

You've now walked through the *entire invention process*, from identifying a problem to developing a working prototype.

Keep in mind:

- *Not all ideas work out the first time.*
- *Creativity and cost-efficiency* go hand in hand.
- *Your mind is your most powerful tool*—train it, trust it, and use it well.

Welcome to the world of invention.

In the next chapter, we'll explore the specific steps of the invention process—from ideation to execution, protection, and beyond.

4

Protecting Your Invention

An idea not protected is an opportunity surrendered.

The Value of Protection

An invention holds little commercial or strategic value if it is not adequately protected under intellectual property law. While creating a novel product or process is a significant achievement, it does not automatically confer ownership or exclusivity. Without legal protection, anyone can replicate, use, or profit from your invention without your permission. Worse still, another party could file for patent rights on your idea, potentially excluding you entirely. Leaving an invention unprotected is akin to leaving a bag of money unattended in a public space, making it vulnerable and easily taken.

Securing a Patent

So, how do we protect an invention?

The most effective method is by securing a *patent*. A granted patent gives you the legal right to exclude others from making, using, or selling your invention. This exclusive right lasts for 20 years from the date of filing. During this time, you can:

- Manufacture and sell the product without competition
- License your invention to others for royalties
- Sell the patent outright for a profit

> A granted patent gives you the legal right to exclude others from making, using, or selling your invention.

Once the 20 years are up, the invention enters the public domain. Until then, if well protected, a good patent can feel like sitting on a gold mine.

The Patent Process: A Reality Check

Coming up with a great invention is hard. *Getting a patent for it is even harder.* The process is often long, costly, and complex. Most inventors work with a *patent attorney*, who files the application on their behalf. However, this does not mean your job is over.

You must work closely with your attorney to:

- Ensure the invention is fully understood
- Include every essential detail
- Frame strong, broad claims

A well-prepared patent application is a collaboration between the inventor and attorney.

Prior Art Search

Before filing for a patent, you must perform a *prior art search*—a detailed examination of existing inventions and publications to determine if your idea is truly original.

A thorough prior art search involves reviewing existing patents, publications, and products to identify potential overlaps. Even if similarities are found, minor but significant differences in design, process, or function may still allow for patentability. Identifying these differences can help refine and strengthen your invention.

"Not finding a match in prior art is like winning the lottery."

Many inventors wrongly assume their idea is unique. Don't be surprised to find an almost identical invention already patented or published.

If you do find similar work:

- Analyze the differences
- Identify any unique features in your idea
- Consider modifying your invention to avoid infringement

This is an essential part of strengthening your future patent application.

It is important to re-evaluate your invention and conduct new searches each time you make adjustments. In some cases, variations uncovered during development may constitute new inventions themselves and should be considered for separate patent filings or included as part of a broader claim strategy

Variations and Broader Claims

During product development, you may explore different versions or variations of your idea. Even if these seem minor, *document every variation*. Why?

The reasons why these variations should be included in your patent are:

- Broadens your protection

- Prevents competitors from exploiting gaps
- Makes your patent harder to circumvent

Avoid the mistake of protecting only your "best" version—leave nothing on the table.

The Concept of "Picket Fence" Patents

In an industry, it's common to file *additional patents* around a core invention. These "picket fence" patents protect variations that:

- You may not plan to produce
- Still hold strategic value in blocking competitors

This layered protection strategy helps maintain a strong market position.

Documenting the Invention

Before you even approach a patent attorney, prepare a *comprehensive invention disclosure document*. This includes:

- A clear description of the invention (with drawings/photos)
- Purpose and background of the invention (the problem it solves and how it improves upon existing solutions)
- First conception date and witness information (if any)
- All test results, Tables, and data comparisons
- Documentation of prior art search and your analysis

This document will help your attorney evaluate and draft the patent effectively. Additionally, it serves as evidence of the invention's development timeline, which may be relevant in legal disputes or patent office reviews.

Attorney's Role in the Prior Art Search

Even after your own search, your patent attorney will conduct a broader one. Often, new prior art will be uncovered. You may need to:

- Adjust your design again
- Go through multiple rounds of revision

Don't lose hope—many inventions survive this process stronger than ever.

Writing the Patent Application

Once cleared, your attorney will begin drafting the application. It typically includes:

- Abstract summarizing of the invention
- Background and related prior art
- Description of the invention
- Supporting data and test results
- *Claims*—the heart of the patent

Understanding Patent Claims

Claims are the most critical part of your patent. They define *exactly what is protected*. There are three types:

1. *Independent Claims*: Stand-alone statements that define the core invention (the most critical and carry the highest value).
2. *Dependent Claims*: Build upon independent claims by specifying additional features (these offer narrower protection).
3. *Design Claims*: Protect the ornamental appearance of a product based solely on illustrations, offering limited coverage.
4. *Tip:* A strong patent will have multiple independent claims with broad language. Inventors should participate closely during the claim-drafting phase, ensuring all key features and variations are captured. Experienced inventors often contribute directly to claim language in order to maximize coverage and strategic value.

The Power of Language

The strength of a patent lies in its claims. Poorly written claims can render even a groundbreaking invention vulnerable to imitation.

Let's consider an example:

- Weak claim: "*A structure with four layers of films laminated together.*"

    This phrasing restricts protection to only the four-layered version. Competitors could legally produce three- or five-layered variants that function similarly, bypassing the patent.
- Stronger claim: "*A structure with at least two layers of films laminated together.*"

    This language offers greater protection by encompassing a wider range of potential designs, including all versions the inventor tested.

Patent language must be carefully constructed to anticipate and prevent design-arounds. Subtle changes in language make all the difference in fending off competition.

Thinking Like the Competition

When writing claims, *think like a rival* trying to bypass your patent. Identify vulnerabilities and close them. Sometimes, you don't need to change the product—just the wording of the claims to cover a wider range.

Hypothetical Example: The Chair

Inventors often seek to design around existing patents. The success of this strategy depends on how the original claims are written.

Suppose someone holds a patent on "a chair with four legs".

- You could file a patent for a chair with *three legs*—a different structure.
- A five-legged chair, however, may still *infringe* the original four-leg patent. (Cross-licensing agreements may be needed to allow mutual use of patented technologies.)

How the claims are written and interpreted is of prime importance. This example shows the complexity of patent overlaps and why legal expertise is essential.

Collaborating with Your Attorney

Collaboration with a patent attorney is vital to securing strong intellectual property rights. While the attorney will manage the legal language and formatting of the application, your input ensures the technical accuracy and strategic breadth of the claims.

Your role doesn't end once the attorney gets involved. On the contrary, you must:

- Share all test data, models, and prototypes
- Be proactive in the development of the claim
- Help draft or revise the claim's language

This collaborative process often leads to stronger patents and wider protection.

Before You File: Crucial Warnings

- *Keep Your Invention Confidential*: Public disclosure before filing can eliminate your right to patent.
- *Don't Market Prematurely*: Even showcasing your idea can put your protection at risk.
- *Company Policies Apply*: If employed, your company may have partial or full rights to your invention.

If you must share the invention (for example, with potential customers or internal teams), use non-disclosure agreements (NDAs) to safeguard confidentiality. These agreements allow you to evaluate market potential or justify development costs without compromising patent rights.

Also, be mindful of *first-to-file* rules. The law in the US now grants patents to the first applicant, not necessarily the first inventor. Prompt filing is essential to securing rights, especially in competitive industries where similar ideas may arise simultaneously.

Different countries have different rules—*know your jurisdiction* before taking action.

Navigating the Patent Process

Filing a Patent Application for a Product vs. a Process

There are multiple ways to file a patent application, depending on the nature of your invention. When you invent something, you may end up with not only a product but also a unique process to manufacture it. Ideally, you should file a *patent application for both*—the product and the process. However, depending on the nature of the invention, the patent office may request you to file two separate applications: one for the product and one for the process.

If you are forced to choose between the two, *always prioritize the product patent*. Here's why:

- *Product patents are more valuable.* They allow you to stop others from making or selling your invention, regardless of how it was made.
- *Process patents are limited.* They protect only the specific method used. Someone else could legally create the same product using a different process.

It's also *easier to detect infringement* on a product patent—often, just by inspecting the product itself. In contrast, identifying how something was made is incredibly difficult without direct access to a competitor's manufacturing process. This makes process patents *harder to police* and more vulnerable to infringement without detection.

For this reason, many companies *avoid filing process patents* unless there's a way to prove how something was made. In such cases, the process is instead *guarded as a trade secret*.

Inventorship: Who Gets Credit

A critical rule in patent law is that *all inventors who contributed to the invention* must be named in the application. Leaving someone out—intentionally or not—can lead to legal complications. Conversely, you *cannot include anyone* who didn't directly contribute.

If you are the only inventor, only your name will appear. If there are multiple inventors, the *primary inventor is listed first*, followed by the others. In many cases, especially in formal documentation, you might see the lead inventor's name followed by "et al.", meaning "and others."

Filing a Patent Application

Once your patent application is ready, your attorney will file it with the USPTO. Be prepared for the fact that the process can be *costly*.

- *Typical US filing costs*: ~$25,000
- *Foreign applications*: up to $50,000, depending on the countries
- *Low-budget filings*: As low as $5,000 with individual or budget services

The filing cost varies based on the *number of claims* in your application. Once submitted, it can take about *18 months* before you receive any response from the USPTO.

During the pending period, you are allowed—and encouraged—to mark your product as *"Patent Pending"*. While this label does not provide enforceable rights, it serves as a public notice that a patent application has been filed and that, upon approval, others may be liable for infringement dating back to the grant date.

Processing the Patent Application

Filing does *not guarantee approval*. Your application is assigned to a *patent examiner* who reviews your invention for:

- *Novelty*
- *Usefulness*
- *Non-obviousness*

The examiner conducts a *prior art search* and may interpret your claims differently than you or your attorney. One common reason for rejection is the belief that your invention is *obvious to a person having ordinary skill in the art.*

Common Realities in the Patent Process

- *Most applications receive an initial rejection.*
- *Only 3 percent* of my own patents were approved on the first try.
- *Arguments and counterarguments* with the examiner are routine.
- You may need to *conduct more research or refine your claims* to move forward.

An examiner's interpretation often becomes a point of contention between the applicant and the examiner. In most cases, the first communication from the patent office is a rejection—either partial or total—of your claims.

Responding to Rejections

A rejection is not the end of the road. Rejections can be *partial* (for some claims) or *complete*. Minor rejections may be easily overcome.

You and your attorney will have the opportunity to respond with counterarguments, clarifications, or claim amendments. Your attorney will review the examiner's arguments and prepare a *formal response*. Your active involvement during this phase is crucial, as only you possess detailed knowledge of your invention and its development. Often, overlooked details can be pivotal in overcoming an examiner's objections.

You and your attorney may go through *multiple rounds of rebuttals,* and in some cases, receive a *final rejection*.

But this doesn't mean it's over as you can intensively revise your claim and make sure a review is done.

Appeals and Interviews

You can appeal against a final rejection to the *patent appeal board*, which reviews both sides before making a decision. I've had two such cases, and both were ultimately granted after appeal.

Another strategy is to *request an in-person interview* with the examiner. Though rare, it can be highly effective. I once presented a *physical model* of my invention compared to the cited prior art. That visual comparison convinced the examiner, and my patent was granted shortly after.

Granting the Patent

If your arguments succeed, the patent is *granted*. You'll receive the official grant date, and your patent will be valid for *20 years from the filing date*.

This gives you the *exclusive right* to make, use, and sell your invention. From that point on, you can enforce your rights against infringers.

While *legal action* is an option, often a *formal cease-and-desist letter* from your attorney is sufficient. Be aware, however, that asserting your patent can be *costly and time-consuming*, especially against large corporations.

A well-known case is *Robert Kearns vs. Ford Motor Company*, over intermittent windshield wipers. After a long battle, Kearns won a significant amount of compensation. There are many such stories of solo inventors standing up to giants.

Invalidating a Granted Patent

Although a rare occurrence, a patent can be *invalidated*. This typically happens when a *threatening patent* is granted, but *overlooks existing prior art* that's already in the public domain.

If you can prove this prior art existed—and was overlooked or dismissed by the examiner—you can challenge the validity of the granted patent. However, this process is *long, expensive,* and *uncertain*.

Other Ways to Protect Your Invention

Not all inventions are patented. There are valid reasons to *skip patent filing*:

- *Difficulty in detecting infringement, especially with process inventions*
- *High costs of enforcement and filing*
- *The invention is difficult to reverse engineer.*

Filing a patent makes all your details public—including to your competition. If they believe they can get away with copying, they might try.

Trade Secrets

An alternative is to protect your invention as a *trade secret*. Trade secrets do not require registration but depend entirely on your ability to keep the information confidential. This works best if:

- Your invention is *hard to reverse-engineer*
- You can *safely guard the details*

One of the most famous examples is the *Coca-Cola formula*, considered the world's most tightly guarded secret,stored in a secure vault in Atlanta.

The downside? If someone independently invents the same thing, they can patent or use it freely.

Pre-emptive Disclosure

If you're not ready to use or patent an invention but want to prevent others from claiming it, consider *publishing it*—in a place your competitors are unlikely to find. This creates *prior art*, blocking others from obtaining a patent on the same concept.

To Summarize

Protecting your invention is not just a legal necessity—it's a strategic move to turn your creativity into lasting value. While the process can be complex and demanding, securing robust intellectual property rights ensures that your efforts, creativity, and investments are not lost to opportunistic competitors. By conducting diligent prior art searches, documenting your work thoroughly, collaborating closely with experienced patent attorneys, and crafting broad and strategic claims, you can transform your invention into a well-defended, commercially valuable asset. A great idea without protection is simply an opportunity left vulnerable.

Protecting your invention is a complex decision—*patents, trade secrets,* and *strategic disclosures,* each have advantages and trade-offs. Understanding the nuances of the patent process empowers you to make the best decision for your invention, budget, and business strategy.

5

Building the Foundation of a Young Inventor

Invention Begins with the Right Mindset

None of us are born inventors. Inventive traits evolve as we grow. Still, we are born with some essential qualities—*ambition, imagination, motivation, inspiration,* and *persistence*—even if only in the form of a seed. If these traits are identified early, nurtured thoughtfully, and applied consistently, they can shape a future inventor. Over time, we mature to tackle challenges in meaningful ways. The attitudes we develop during our early years profoundly influence our future success.

Consider how young children respond to challenges such as assembling shape and color puzzles. Some give up after a single failed attempt. Others persist slightly longer, only to abandon the task in frustration. But a few show remarkable patience, continuing to try until the puzzle is solved. These early behaviors often foreshadow how individuals will face challenges later in life.

A Humble Beginning: Life in Kumbalanghy

I was born in *Kerala*, in the southwest corner of India—a state known as "God's Own Country". My childhood home was in

Kumbalanghy, a six-square-mile island village, serene and isolated, filled with coconut palms, mango trees, and exotic birds.

During my early years, the village had no electricity, paved roads, or motor vehicles. Yet it was here, in the midst of simplicity, that the seeds of invention and creativity were sown in me. Despite the lack of material luxuries, I never felt deprived. My family ensured we had life's necessities, but more importantly, they provided me with the freedom to think independently and act creatively. I considered it a privilege to make the most of what I had, and I learned early on how to turn limitations into opportunities.

My childhood was a tapestry of adventure, curiosity, and fulfillment. We lived in a modest home facing a beautiful waterfront, where the rising sun greeted us every morning. At the time, I took the natural beauty of my village for granted. Only after moving away and returning years later, did I truly appreciate its peacefulness and visual splendor. A photograph I took during one of those return visits—of the very sunrise I once ignored—now hangs in my New Jersey home, reminding me daily of my roots.

Over the years, I have traveled to more than 25 countries, but I have yet to find a place as tranquil and inspiring as my childhood home. What was once an isolated village has since transformed into one of Kerala's premier tourist destinations. Yet even in its earlier, undeveloped state, Kumbalanghy was fertile ground for growing imaginative and determined minds.

Today, Kumbalanghy is a modern resort and one of Kerala's top tourist attractions. But the values and lessons from my childhood remain timeless.

A Village Marked by Remarkable Achievements

Kumbalanghy, with a population of just 25,000 at the time, produced an unusually high number of successful professionals—scientists, doctors, engineers, lawyers, politicians, clergy, and educators—

surpassing neighboring towns in distinction and achievement. The village sent more students abroad for higher education than many larger communities. One of my closest childhood friends, Professor K.V. Thomas, went on to serve as a Member of Parliament and a Cabinet Minister in the Indian government.

Family and Faith: The Support System

I was the 10th child in a family of 11. You'd expect that such a position would come with little attention, but in a family of that size, no one had it all to themselves. We were close-knit, energetic, and always looking out for each other.

My parents, Paul and Treesa, were loving yet disciplined. As devout Catholics, they insisted on daily Mass and taught us integrity, compassion, and service. I still remember how my father invited a hungry beggar home after church, and my mother prepared him a hot meal. That simple act of kindness left a lifelong impression on me.

Discipline was firm. When my brother was bitten by a dog, my father assumed he must have provoked it and grounded him for the day. While strict, this upbringing prepared me to face future challenges with resilience and strength.

Living Without: A Catalyst for Creativity

Without electricity in the village, our nights were lit by kerosene lamps. Travel was minimal and roads unpaved. Our main transportation was by boat, bicycle, or rickshaw—a two-wheeled cart pulled by a person. I was fascinated by these rickshaws and admired how the drivers constantly improved them to stand out and provide better comfort and safety. The rickshaw, with its large wheels and convertible roof, greatly interested me as a child. Some rickshaw drivers added features like rain curtains, improved seats, and even reflective lights. One creative operator invented a braking system, sharing it with others in the community. They didn't invent the rickshaw, but they made it better—as a true grassroots innovation.

These daily encounters with creative problem-solving planted a seed in me. I saw that *invention doesn't always begin in labs—it can start on dirt roads with just basic needs and curious minds.*

Lighting the Way: Early Ingenuity

Studying at night with a kerosene lamp wasn't ideal, but we made it work. While some might see this as a hindrance to creativity, I viewed it as a challenge. Flashlights were a luxury few could afford. Yet, even in this dark environment, our minds were lit with *imagination* and *resourcefulness*.

Our environment was rich with opportunities for improvement and innovation. Every day presented a new problem to solve, a process to work on to make it better, or a product to enhance.

We connected to the outside world through a newspaper delivered on foot. I would rush to read it, eager to know what was happening beyond our small island. This curiosity became the fuel for innovation. My first visit to a nearby town introduced me to cars and buses, which seemed magical compared to our village rickshaws. I returned determined to *imitate, improve,* and *experiment.*

Childhood Inventions: Playtime as Practice

Before I started school, my friends and I had no access to store-bought toys. But this limitation led us to invent our own. With no toy stores available for us, we created our own toys, using local materials.

The Leaf Whistle: An Early Prototyping Lesson

One of my earliest creations was a whistle made from a large, heart-shaped leaf. By carefully rolling it and adjusting the tightness, I discovered I could produce sounds that mimicked the musical notes played on my friend's store-bought bamboo flute. The simplicity of the leaf whistle opened my imagination—it proved that everyday materials could be transformed into something functional with just a little ingenuity.

Encouraged by this discovery, I decided to take on the greater challenge of making a bamboo flute of my own. My first attempts, however, were frustrating. Using only a knife, I tried carving holes into the bamboo, but no matter how carefully I worked, the flute would not produce a clean sound. At first, I assumed my lack of skill was the problem. But after studying my friend's flute more closely, I noticed something important: the holes were not cut, but burned. That single observation changed everything.

Armed with this insight, I experimented with a candle flame to burn the holes into the bamboo. The fire allowed me to create cleaner, rounder openings that resonated properly. I then refined the holes with my knife to adjust pitch and tone. When I finally blew into the finished flute and heard distinct notes echo back, it felt like a defining moment—I had turned failure into success by observing, experimenting, and refining my approach.

Looking back, this was more than just a childhood project; it was an early lesson in prototyping. I had followed the essential steps every inventor must embrace:

- *Start with a simple idea* (a leaf whistle).
- *Attempt a prototype,* even if crude or imperfect (the first bamboo flute with carved holes).

- *Study existing solutions* to identify what makes them work (realizing the holes were burned).
- *Iterate and refine* by testing a new method (using fire and then shaping with a knife).
- *Achieve a working model*, not perfect, but functional and meaningful.

This process mirrors the journey of countless inventors—transforming observation and failure into learning, and learning into innovation. My bamboo flute was not just a toy; it was my first true prototype.

The Two-wheel Cart: An Early Innovation

Among the many childhood toys fashioned from nature, one of my favorites was a simple two-wheel cart. Its wheels were made from small baby coconuts, while the axles came from the strong, flexible ribs of coconut leaves. A string, twisted from the stalks of coconut fronds, served as the pull cord. It was crude but effective—the cart rolled smoothly across the dirt paths, providing endless entertainment.

But as with most inventions, curiosity soon demanded improvement. I began experimenting with ways to make the cart look and function differently. The first modification was to expand the design into a four-wheel version. Instead of being just a rolling platform, this new cart had a box-like body constructed from sticks and covered in mango leaves. It was no longer just a toy to pull; it began to resemble a miniature vehicle—a symbol of imagination transforming play into innovation.

The true leap forward came when I borrowed inspiration from another toy, a bird that spun in circles when powered by a twisted rubber band. I thought, "*If rubber bands could create motion in a bird toy, why not apply the same idea to my cart?*" I tied a rubber band to the axle, twisted it, and released it. To my delight, the cart moved on its own—a primitive but genuine self-propelled vehicle.

Although such toys already existed elsewhere, building one with my own hands carried far greater meaning. It was not about creating something new to the world, but about *creating something new to me*. That distinction is crucial: innovation often begins not with a revolutionary breakthrough, but with reimagining and reapplying existing principles in a new context.

This little cart taught me several early lessons about innovation:

- *Curiosity drives improvement*: The two-wheel cart was fun, but I couldn't resist wondering what else it could become.
- *Observation sparks ideas*: Watching how the rubber-band bird worked gave me the idea to add propulsion.
- *Trial and error leads to progress*: Many early versions failed—the rubber band slipped, the axle bent, the cart veered off course—but each mistake pushed me closer to a working model.
- *Innovation is personal*: Even if others had made similar toys, the act of inventing my own version gave me confidence in my creativity and problem-solving.

In hindsight, I was already applying the basic principles of engineering—though at the time I had no idea what "engineering" even meant. I was experimenting, observing, iterating, and improving. This was innovation in its purest, most natural form: a child transforming curiosity into creation.

Lessons from the Two-wheel Cart

This childhood toy may seem simple, but it illustrates many of the same principles that drive modern innovation. Here's how:

Step	What I Did as a Child	Innovation Principle
Start with what you have	Built a two-wheel cart from coconuts, leaf ribs, and stalks.	Resourcefulness: using available materials to create solutions.
Seek improvement	Added more wheels and a leaf-covered body to make it resemble a car.	Curiosity and iteration: improving on the original design.
Borrow ideas from elsewhere	Adapted the rubber-band mechanism from a spinning bird toy.	Cross-pollination: applying ideas from one field to another.
Test and refine	Faced problems like slipping bands and bent axles, then fixed them.	Trial and error: refining through failures and adjustments.
Celebrate progress	Built a working self-propelled cart.	Confidence: success builds belief in one's creative ability.

Key Takeaway

Innovation doesn't always mean inventing something entirely new. Sometimes, it means *observing, adapting,* and *improving* existing ideas in ways that feel new and meaningful to you. Every small success builds the foundation for greater creative achievements.

Self-winding Paper Alligator

During the summer, I set out to design a new toy, drawing inspiration from a previous project—a wind-up car I had built. I began by constructing a two-wheel axle and attaching it to a rubber band to form the core of a wind-up mechanism. To enhance the design, I introduced a string tied to the axle. As the axle unwound, the string coiled around it, and when pulled, the tension caused the axle to rewind automatically. This innovation allowed the toy to operate independently without requiring manual rewinding after each use.

Inspired by the success of this mechanism, I decided to create a new toy—a paper alligator. I fashioned the head from cardboard, attaching it securely to the axle. I then threaded the string through a small hole at the top of the head, anchoring it with a piece of cardboard to prevent slippage. For the body, I folded a long strip of paper in a fan-like V-shape and attached one end to the head. By compressing the paper at the back, I shaped a tail, completing the alligator's form.

> Innovation doesn't always mean inventing something entirely new. Sometimes, it means *observing, adapting,* and *improving* existing ideas in ways that feel new and meaningful to you.

When the string was pulled and released, the alligator moved forward across the floor. The folded paper body flexed side to side with each motion, closely mimicking the natural movement of a real alligator. Thanks to the automatic rewinding system, the toy was ready for repeated use without the need to reset the mechanism manually.

The toy quickly became a hit among my friends, all eager to try it. My family was impressed—not only was the alligator imaginative and entertaining, but it also functioned on par with commercially available toys. Reflecting on the experience, I now recognize that this idea had real entrepreneurial potential. At the time, I was too young to understand what it meant to be an entrepreneur, but the project clearly demonstrated creativity, innovation, and functional design.

Homemade Candle: A Childhood Innovation in Sustainability

Growing up in a devout Catholic household, one of our cherished daily rituals was our evening prayer before dinner. Our prayer room was adorned with images of Jesus and Mother Mary, and each night we lit candles in reverence. When I was in the third grade, my father entrusted me with the responsibility of lighting and extinguishing the candle—an honor I accepted with great enthusiasm.

One evening, I recalled how tall candles in churches were extinguished, by using a long stick with a cone-shaped tip—a candle snuffer. Inspired by this, I set out to create my own. I crafted a simple snuffer using a sturdy stick from our backyard and a metal kitchen funnel. That night, I waited quietly behind my family during prayer, and at the end, without leaving my place, I reached forward with my homemade snuffer and gently extinguished the candle. My family was both surprised and proud of the thoughtful tool I had created.

Later, I was given the task of cleaning hardened wax from the metal plates beneath the candles—a tedious chore, as the wax was difficult to remove. In search of a better method, I left the plates outside and returned to find the heat of the sun had softened the wax, making it easy to peel off. Intrigued, I collected the wax into a ball and began shaping it with my hands. Over the following days, I experimented with leaving the wax in the sun longer, molding it into different forms, and even melting it, by using a kerosene lamp.

Motivated by curiosity, I decided to attempt making a candle from scratch. I fashioned a mold, using a hollow bamboo stick from our backyard, sealed one end with cardboard, and threaded a wick through the center, securing it to a small rod at the top. I melted the salvaged wax and carefully poured it into the mold. After allowing it to cool in a water bath, I successfully produced a fully functional homemade candle.

That night, during prayer, I lit only one candle—the one I had crafted myself. It was a moment of quiet pride.

Without realizing it, I had engaged in practices now widely promoted as environmentally responsible: recycling, reusing, and minimizing waste. At the time, I was simply making use of what was available. I didn't know the word "sustainability", nor had I heard of "recycling", but reusing the wax seemed like the most natural and efficient approach. What began as a simple act of creativity became an early lesson in resourcefulness and environmental consciousness—an experience that continues to influence my mindset today.

Learning to Swim: An Inventor's Journey

As a child, I often watched my older brothers and their friends swim effortlessly in the lake near our home. Their laughter and freedom in the water stirred a deep *ambition* in me—a determination to join them despite not knowing how to swim. I refused to accept being left behind, and that ambition drove me to search for solutions.

My first attempts were simple and experimental. I tried floating on small pieces of wood, only to discover they sank under my weight. Rather than giving up, I applied *imagination* by experimenting with larger pieces, testing and learning through trial and error. Each failed attempt became a stepping stone, sharpening my understanding of what would—or would not—work.

The breakthrough came when I noticed our gallon-sized aluminum water pots. Lightweight, hollow, and buoyant when inverted, they offered a new possibility. Though I did not understand the science of displacement or buoyancy at the time, I was guided by *inspiration*—the sudden recognition that the trapped air inside these pots could hold me afloat. Acting on this insight, I crafted practical adaptations: tying ropes around the pot to make handles, and even adding arm loops so I could float hands-free. What began as a playful observation evolved into a functional invention.

This early device gave me the confidence to join my brothers in the deep water. Over time, I shed the floating aid and learned to swim freely. Yet my *motivation* pushed me further—I wanted not only to swim, but to test my limits. When a friend challenged me to cross the mile-wide lake and return, I embraced it as an opportunity to prove my persistence. Secretly, I trained for weeks, conditioning my body and building endurance.

On the day of the attempt, I set off alone, my pot-float serving as a safety net. Stroke by stroke, hour after hour, I pressed forward. The journey was exhausting, but my persistence carried me across and back. When I finally reached the shore, weary but victorious, I had achieved something I had once thought impossible. I returned home quietly, never telling my parents, though years later some of my siblings discovered the story and were astonished.

Looking back, this experience was more than learning to swim—it was my first lesson in invention. *Ambition* gave me the drive to begin, *imagination* allowed me to experiment with ideas, *inspiration* revealed a solution in everyday objects, *motivation* fueled my desire to improve, and *persistence* ensured I overcame obstacles. Together, these qualities not only helped me cross a lake but also foreshadowed the mindset that would later define my journey as an inventor.

Home Movie Without Electricity: Thinking Like an Inventor

Growing up in a village without electricity meant we lived with limits most people today could hardly imagine. Yet as children, we didn't feel deprived—we adapted, improvised, and created entertainment from what we had. The only electric device in our home was a flashlight, reserved for emergencies. To me, however, it was a mysterious object full of possibility. I played with it often, even mischievously once, placing it in my mouth and frightening the neighborhood kids with my glowing face. Though I quickly apologized, that moment revealed something deeper: I was already curious about how light could be manipulated.

Our first real taste of modern entertainment came when my uncle, "Uncle BA", built a rustic movie theater powered by a kerosene generator. The projector's whirring beam of light captured my imagination more than the film itself. I was fascinated not only by what I saw on the screen, but by *how* the images moved, how the light transformed still frames into motion. My mind, like that of a budding inventor, immediately began asking: *"Could I recreate this at home with the few resources I had?"*

I began collecting discarded film fragments, studying them like precious artifacts. In a darkened room, I experimented with my flashlight, holding the film in its beam to cast images on the wall. The first results were crude, but they sparked a flood of ideas. With *imagination* guiding me, I cut a square hole in a piece of cardboard to hold a single film frame steady, allowing me to advance the strip slowly by hand. For the first time, I saw the illusion of motion—created not in a theater, but in my own home.

The challenge then became brightness. I soon realized the flashlight's beam was too weak. Inspired by sunlight's intensity, I replaced the flashlight with a mirror angled to reflect the sun into the room. To focus the light, I built a cardboard window with a narrow opening, channeling the beam directly through the film. The result was astonishing: a crisp, bright image appeared on the wall. That day, I staged my first "movie show" without a single wire or electric current. My family and friends gathered in amazement as I projected scenes from scraps of discarded film, powered only by sunlight and curiosity.

It was a defining moment in my childhood. More than just a playful experiment, it was an early exercise in *ambition, imagination,* and *persistence*—the qualities of an inventor in the making. I had taken a simple problem—no access to electricity—and transformed it into an opportunity for innovation. In that moment, I learned an invaluable truth: invention begins not with resources, but with a mind determined to explore possibilities.

The Visionary Manger

As a young boy, the Christmas season always filled me with anticipation—not only for celebration, but also for creation. In our village, families built outdoor mangers as part of the holiday tradition. Most were simple, rustic cribs set in straw. But I wanted mine to be different. I dreamed not only of a manger, but of an entire *modern town* built around it—a place where the sacred story of Bethlehem was reimagined with the conveniences of a world that had not yet reached us.

In my imagination, the holy night unfolded in a village resembling our own, but with *electric streetlights, paved roads, a public park, a water fountain,* and *even systems for water conservation.* At the heart of this futuristic Bethlehem stood a humble manger surrounded by cattle, where a statue of Baby Jesus would rest. My vision was not historically accurate, nor did I intend it to be. Instead, it was a child's attempt to blend reverence with innovation—an exploration of what might happen if tradition met progress.

Since school exams ended only days before Christmas, I began building my project two months in advance. I constructed a raised wooden platform nearly 40 square feet in size and layered it with wet sand. This became the foundation of my town. To represent agriculture, I created rice paddy fields. With my father's help, I soaked rice seeds and planted them weeks ahead of Christmas, timing their growth so that by the special day they would stand like lush miniature crops.

I wanted the streets to look paved, not sandy. I improvised by mixing rice flour, water, and black ink from a fountain pen—my homemade "asphalt". When it dried, the streets had a realistic dark finish, unlike any other manger in the neighborhood.

My biggest challenge was lighting. We had no electricity in the village, but I was determined to create glowing streetlights. With small bulbs, flashlight batteries, and thin wires, I built tiny lamp posts from wooden sticks. I wired them together, concealing the connections behind the structure, and rigged a simple switch from a rubber band. When I flipped it, the bulbs lit up the scene, as though electricity had finally reached our village.

But the centerpiece of my invention was the *working water fountain*, made without a single motor or electric pump. I devised a gravity-fed system by suspending a bucket of water from a tree branch. A rubber hose carried the water downward into a nozzle made from a pen cap. At first, the flow was too strong, but by carefully piercing a tiny hole with a heated needle, I created a pinhole jet that sent water about a foot into the air. To control the stream, I built a clamp valve from scrap metal and rubber bands. With one bucket, the fountain ran for almost two hours—long enough to astonish my family and neighbors.

Each year, I expanded my design. I added *colored bulbs wrapped in translucent paper*, experimented with dyed water for the fountain, and even placed small lights beneath the stream for a glowing nighttime effect. One year, I devised a *recycling system*: a hidden reservoir collected the fountain's water and channeled it through buried tubes to irrigate the rice paddy, creating a primitive sprinkler system. At the time, my goal was simply to save effort in refilling, but in hindsight, it was an early lesson in *sustainability and water conservation*.

What began as a child's playful project soon became a community attraction. Neighbors and friends gathered to admire the glowing streets, the flowing fountain, and the miniature rice fields. Many praised the ingenuity, some tried to imitate it, and I felt a deep sense of pride.

Looking back, I realize this was more than just a Christmas display—it was an expression of a young inventor's *ambition to dream big, imagination to design beyond limits, persistence to overcome challenges, and inspiration to bring joy to others*. That manger was not only a tribute to tradition but also an early glimpse of the way invention can light up even the simplest of settings.

Reflections: Inventor Qualities in the Manger Project

This childhood manger was more than a holiday tradition—it was a living workshop where the essential qualities of an inventor came to life.

- *Ambition*: I did not settle for an ordinary manger. My vision was bold—to design an entire modern town around it, with innovations no one had attempted before.
- *Imagination*: I pictured electric lights, fountains, and even water recycling in a village that had no electricity or plumbing, showing how creativity allows us to see what does not yet exist.
- *Motivation*: The project required weeks of preparation, from planting rice seeds to wiring tiny light bulbs. My motivation was fueled by the joy of building something extraordinary for my family and community.
- *Inspiration*: Watching my uncle power a projector with a kerosene generator and seeing how others built their mangers sparked new ideas. Inspiration turned observation into action.
- *Persistence*: Many attempts failed at first: the pen cap fountain sprayed uncontrollably, the "asphalt" mixture needed adjusting, and the bulbs often burned out. Yet, through trial and error, I refined each detail until it worked.

Together, these qualities transformed a simple manger into an imaginative display that delighted others and foreshadowed the inventive journey I would later pursue in life.

School Days

I attended our village school, which provided education from the first to the 10th grade. The environment was highly disciplined, and by today's standards, it would likely be considered excessively strict. Teachers enforced discipline through a combination of physical and verbal punishments for a range of infractions, including tardiness, lack of attentiveness, incomplete homework, incorrect answers, or general misbehavior. Humiliation was not uncommon, and this created a climate of anxiety and apprehension. I vividly remember experiencing intense nervousness each morning on my way to school, particularly fearful of being sent to the headmaster's office for being late. His typical form of discipline involved making students kneel on coarse gravel spread over concrete—a punishment I endured on more than one occasion.

Among the faculty, however, there was one teacher who stood out due to his unconventional approach. His philosophy was centered on uninterrupted teaching. To avoid constant disruptions and punishments during class, he would begin each session by asking all students to stand and receive pre-emptive discipline, using a bamboo stick. The number of strikes varied, depending on each student's behavior and past performance. Fortunately, I was among those who received minimal punishment. At the time, this approach seemed normal to us, shaped by the rigid standards of the day.

Despite the militaristic style of education, the school produced an extraordinary number of professionals—doctors, engineers, lawyers, educators, clergy, and community leaders—surpassing the achievements of many neighboring schools. Attending our 50th high school reunion, I was proud to see so many of my classmates holding prominent and successful positions. Looking back, I attribute two critical qualities to that education: it instilled resilience and the confidence to face challenges head-on.

Fantasy: Towards Setting Higher Goals

Growing up without access to television or radio, our primary source of news was the daily newspaper. Occasionally, we gained a glimpse of the broader world through newsreels shown before movies in local theaters—rare experiences for me. These short films often featured dignitaries and celebrities descending from airplanes, greeted by applauding crowds. Their sharp attire—suits, ties, and sunglasses—left a lasting impression on me. From a young age, I dreamed of one day traveling by an airplane and being welcomed like a celebrity. Ironically, at that time, I had never even ridden in a car.

In high school, my wardrobe consisted of shorts and short-sleeved shirts. I had never worn trousers, a long-sleeved shirt, or even seen a suit and tie in person. One summer, my older brother, Lieutenant K.P. Job, returned home on vacation from the Indian navy. He had traveled widely and often shared fascinating stories about foreign countries and modern conveniences. That summer, I noticed he had packed a formal suit and tie. One day, when no one was around, I tried them on—oversized as they were—and topped off the look with his sunglasses. I stared at myself in the mirror, pretending I was stepping off an airplane and waving to a cheering crowd. For a brief moment, I felt like someone important—a celebrity, even. That experience sparked a powerful desire in me to strive for greatness. From that day forward, I set my goals even higher.

Having Fun: Innovation and Problem-solving

During high school, I spent much of my free time with a small group of spirited friends. One of our favorite, albeit mischievous, pastimes was attempting to pick mangoes from a tall mango tree in the schoolyard. The tree belonged to the church and was strictly off limits, which only added to its allure. We usually waited until the teachers had left before beginning our efforts.

The challenge was significant—the tree was tall, and the ripe mangoes hung at the far tips of the branches, well beyond our reach. One of the boys owned a slingshot, and we took turns throwing small stones in hopes of dislodging the fruit. Despite repeated attempts, we rarely succeeded.

Recognizing the flaw in our method, I experimented with an alternative approach. Instead of using small stones, I placed a longer, heavier stick in the slingshot pocket, guiding it with my fingers to control the trajectory. After a few trial shots, I succeeded in hitting a large cluster of mangoes, causing several to fall at once. My friends quickly adopted the technique, and before long, we had gathered more mangoes than we could possibly eat. In retrospect, I realized I had effectively transformed a simple slingshot into a compact bow-and-arrow mechanism.

Yet, the thrill of success was quickly followed by guilt. As a regular church-goer who attended daily Mass and weekly confession, I admitted my actions during confession. The priest, who was also responsible for managing church property, did not take it lightly. He warned that he might inform my father—a possibility that frightened me enough to abandon our mango-hunting exploits altogether. Looking back, I sometimes reflect humorously on that moment, questioning the absolute sanctity of confidentiality in confession.

This experience taught me an enduring lesson: when conventional methods fail, I instinctively seek alternatives, challenge limitations, and pursue better solutions. That enthusiasm, energy, and willingness to act has consistently led to successful outcomes in my life.

Chemistry Laboratory: Shaping Creativity

I began college at the age of 15, and chemistry quickly became my favorite subject. Fascinated by the magic of chemical reactions, I often performed small experiments at home. On one occasion, I obtained a reagent from the college lab that changed color in the presence of sugar. Intrigued, I tested it with sugar water and imagined its potential as a simple diagnostic tool for diabetes. Because a distant relative was suspected of having the disease, I asked my parents for permission to request a urine sample for testing. Their reaction was swift and firm—they explained that I was unqualified to conduct medical tests and that inaccurate results could have serious consequences. Realizing the gravity of the situation, I immediately abandoned the idea. It was an early reminder that curiosity must always be balanced with responsibility.

Later that year, during my final chemistry exam, we were required to identify two unknown substances labeled *Chemical A* and *Chemical B* and synthesize a byproduct. Chemical A was of good quality and relatively easy to identify. Chemical B, however, was aged and degraded, rendering the standard tests unreliable. After numerous trials and careful reasoning, I narrowed the possibilities to two compounds. Recalling a specialized test that could distinguish between them, I quickly performed it. The result ruled out one candidate, allowing me to identify Chemical B by elimination.

Knowing that the degraded Chemical B would make it nearly impossible to produce the required byproduct, I nevertheless documented every procedure, observation, and the logic behind my conclusions. I also noted the poor condition of the reagent. When the results were announced, I was thrilled to receive an A+ along with a handwritten comment: *"Great work and excellent execution."* My professor valued the clarity of my reasoning and meticulous record-keeping even though the experiment itself did not yield the expected result. That experience boosted my confidence and reinforced a powerful truth: in science—and in life—how you approach a problem can matter as much as the outcome itself.

Lesson Learned

This incident taught me that creativity is not just about bold ideas but about disciplined thinking, curiosity tempered with responsibility, and the willingness to adapt when conditions are unfavorable. Success often depends less on producing a perfect result and more on how carefully you observe, analyze, and communicate your reasoning.

How to Be Creative and Approach Problems Effectively

- *Stay Curious but Responsible*: Let curiosity drive exploration, but recognize ethical and safety boundaries.
- *Think Systematically*: Break complex problems into smaller steps, test one variable at a time, and record your reasoning.
- *Embrace Setbacks as Data*: A failed experiment still yields valuable insights that can guide the next step.
- *Look for Alternatives*: When a direct method fails, step back and consider unconventional paths or indirect indicators.
- *Document and Reflect*: Careful notes and clear logic build credibility and reveal patterns that create new ideas.

Creativity thrives at the intersection of open-mindedness and disciplined analysis. The best solutions often emerge not from a single brilliant leap, but from persistent questioning, flexible thinking, and the courage to explore beyond obvious answers.

Mindset Formed by a Creative Childhood

Though our lives lacked material wealth, we were rich in creativity, community, and curiosity. The environment around me—full of challenges, limitations, and opportunities—became my playground and classroom.

I learned:

- *Imagination thrives when resources are limited.*
- *Curiosity can turn obstacles into opportunities.*
- *Supportive environments—even strict ones—can foster innovation.*
- *Simple acts of kindness can leave the deepest impact.*

For any young mind, this is the key: *start where you are, use what you have, and always stay curious.* The inventor's journey begins not with a blueprint, but with a mindset—and that mindset is shaped long before your first invention sees the light.

The Inventor's Spark

Growing up in a remote village with limited resources may seem like an unlikely beginning for an inventor. Yet, those very constraints became the foundation for creativity, resilience, and a deep appreciation for innovation. Surrounded by nature, supported by family, and driven by curiosity, I learned to view the world not for what it was, but for what it could become. These early experiences helped shape the inventor I would one day become.

6

Attitude

Geared to Invention

A New Life in a New Country

At the age of 19, I earned a Bachelor's degree in chemistry from Sacred Heart College in Kerala, India. Shortly after graduation, I was offered a position as a Junior Lecturer at the same institution, where I was primarily responsible for supervising students in laboratory sessions. After one year in this role, I made a life-changing decision: to pursue higher education in the US.

First Experience Abroad

I arrived in the US in 1967. At the time, traveling abroad for education was uncommon in India. The Indian government permitted travelers to carry only eight US dollars when leaving the country, which meant that individuals had to find their own means of support while abroad. I had the option of traveling by ship or air—an opportunity not afforded to earlier generations. I recall a cousin who immigrated on a ship to the US earlier. His father had given him a bunch of 30 plantains—large, starchy bananas common in India—as sustenance for the month-long voyage. He told me he ate one banana each day and arrived in America just as he consumed the last one.

In contrast, I had the privilege of flying. It was my first flight, and though the experience was new, I felt only excitement. My destination was a college in Manchester, New Hampshire, which required five connecting flights: from Kochi to Mumbai, then to Frankfurt, Germany, and onward to the US. In Frankfurt, the airline provided an overnight stay with dinner. When the waiter offered me a selection of drinks, the only one I recognized was beer. Out of curiosity, I ordered one—only to discover that it was not included in the dinner voucher. The beer cost two dollars—25 per cent of my total savings. That experience taught me a valuable lesson in budgeting, and I resolved not to eat or drink again until I reached my final destination.

Unfortunately, due to flight delays, I missed my connection to Boston and later to Manchester. Stranded late at night in an unfamiliar city, I encountered a woman struggling with heavy luggage. I helped her with her bags, and in gratitude, she inquired about my situation. Although my English was limited, I explained my circumstances. I recalled having met a man at the Kochi airport who had given me the address of his uncle, a priest living in Boston. I mentioned this to the woman, who, coincidentally, lived near that address. She graciously offered to drive me there, ensuring that I arrived safely.

The priest welcomed me warmly. He provided me with dinner and a place to sleep. That night, I felt reassured that I would be able to thrive in this new country, supported by the kindness of strangers and a deep sense of hope.

Graduate Education and Career Foundation

I completed a Master's degree course in chemistry at the University of Massachusetts. Encouraged by a friend to broaden my career prospects, I shifted my focus to chemical engineering and earned a second Master's degree in plastics engineering. This decision significantly expanded my technical knowledge and proved to be a pivotal moment in shaping my professional future. Both degrees were supported by teaching fellowships awarded by the university.

Following my studies, I moved to Canada to pursue new career opportunities.

Canadian Experience

My natural inclination for problem-solving and innovation found fertile ground in the Canadian industry. In this section, I will describe several professional projects and inventions developed in collaboration with colleagues. For each example, I will outline the context, motivation, development approach, outcomes, and key lessons—while omitting confidential or proprietary details. These stories are intended to motivate aspiring inventors, particularly young individuals who may not yet have taken their first steps toward innovation.

Staying Alert to Opportunities

My first job in Canada was with a company that manufactured plastic cups and lids. This transition from academia to industry was eye-opening. I quickly realized that the specific knowledge gained from textbooks was often less important than the process of learning itself. What truly mattered was how we were trained to think critically, adapt as fast as possible, solve problems, and make sound decisions. The confidence and analytical mindset developed during my academic years proved invaluable.

Although I kept my college textbooks in my office for years, I seldom referred to them. The core value of education lay not in memorizing facts, but in applying learned principles to new challenges. My work focused on optimizing plastic processing equipment and resin selection, resulting in improved production efficiency. However, as the company prioritized manufacturing over innovation, I found limited room for growth.

A New Chapter in Innovation

The following year, I joined a larger company specializing in electrical insulation products. My first major project involved developing a cost-effective underground transformer with improved durability. The transformer was encased in a thick molded plastic shell, which served as electrical insulation and protection against impact, corrosion, and environmental damage. I collaborated with an electrical engineer on the redesign, ensuring compatibility between the chemical and electrical components.

The existing plastic formulation was costly, so I analyzed each ingredient's function, properties, and cost. I explored alternative materials within the same chemical families and conducted comparative testing. Ultimately, I developed a new formulation that reduced both the number of ingredients and the processing steps—while also lowering costs and enhancing performance. This was one of the few times I directly applied knowledge gained from my academic studies. It boosted my confidence and extended my expertise beyond chemistry into cross-disciplinary teamwork—an essential trait for any inventor.

I also made it a routine to walk through the manufacturing floor each morning, engaging with machine operators to better understand their challenges and concerns. Though the equipment was outdated, the operations were stable. By questioning the status quo and identifying opportunities for improvement, I was able to propose and implement several process enhancements that led to greater efficiency and product quality. The ability to challenge existing practices is a defining characteristic of a successful inventor.

A Strategic Move to the United States

Despite a fulfilling role in Canada, I realized that the US offered broader opportunities for professional advancement. While attending a seminar in Boston, I met an R&D director from a New Jersey company. After reviewing my experience, he expressed his interest in hiring me, contingent upon securing permanent residency in the US—a process known to be lengthy and uncertain.

After an initial phone interview with the company's president, I received a job offer and an assurance that they would handle the immigration process. However, a year later, immigration officials informed me that my application was still delayed due to a backlog. Disheartened, I communicated the situation to the company and assumed they had lost interest.

To my surprise, I later received a call from the new CEO, who had reviewed my résumé and wanted to meet me. During our interview in Toronto, he expressed his strong interest in my work and confirmed his desire to bring me to the US. I explained the immigration delays, but he assured me that he would manage the process. Within two weeks, I received my visa and relocated to New Jersey with my family.

Continued Innovation in a New Environment

The company specialized in rubber molding and electrical insulation tapes. Once again, I encountered outdated machinery and processes that had remained unchanged for years. Drawing from my recent experience in electrical insulation, I focused on identifying inefficiencies and potential improvements.

By paying close attention to the operations, engaging with employees, and applying my technical expertise, I was able to contribute significantly to the company's product quality and process optimization.

Throughout my journey—from India to the US via Canada—my attitude toward invention has remained grounded in curiosity, problem-solving, collaboration, and a willingness to step beyond my comfort zone. These experiences shaped my career, guided my innovations, and strengthened my belief that invention is not confined to laboratories or workshops—it begins with a mindset and a keen eye for opportunity.

Identifying Opportunity and Pursuing It

Innovation often begins with a problem. Shortly after joining a new company, I encountered a recurring failure in the field: high-temperature insulation tapes were melting or burning during extreme electrical conditions, particularly when high-voltage wire joints were exposed to lightning strikes. These failures left the underlying wires dangerously exposed.

The technical requirement was clear: we needed a tape material capable of withstanding temperatures as high as 3400°F for a minimum of 20 seconds without compromising its insulating properties. This was an ambitious challenge—most polymers and rubbers degrade well below this temperature, and even metals like steel would not survive under such extreme conditions.

I was assigned to this project as a solo researcher. For several months, I tested various rubber and polymer formulations, all of which failed to meet the performance criteria. Each failure, however, provided valuable data. I soon realized that flame-resistant rubber alone would not suffice. I began experimenting with special filler materials, incorporating them into the base formulation. The addition improved performance moderately, but we were still far from our target.

Progress stalled until I altered the ratio of the existing ingredients. This adjustment yielded significant improvements, renewing my optimism. Further trials revealed that the process conditions—temperature, mixing speed, and curing time—played a critical role in the final material properties. I meticulously adjusted each parameter, eventually identifying a precise set of conditions that optimized the formulation's performance.

However, we still lacked a means of reliably testing materials at 3400°F. Fortunately, the University of Connecticut housed a plasma arc test facility capable of simulating a direct lightning strike. Though the test was expensive, I reached out to the university. The professor in charge initially discouraged me, noting that even metals often failed under those conditions and expressing skepticism about testing a rubber-based material.

Despite his doubts, I was committed to moving forward. When I arrived on a Monday morning with my tape samples—three inches wide and a quarter-inch thick—he reiterated his concerns. He wrapped the sample around a lead pipe (which melts at low temperatures) and secured it in the test chamber.

As the plasma arc test began, the tape initially ignited but quickly formed a dense crust on the surface. This unexpected reaction created a protective barrier that resisted the extreme heat. Minutes passed, then 10, then 20—well beyond the required 20-second threshold. The test equipment eventually overheated and had to be shut down, but the tape remained intact. Remarkably, even the lead pipe beneath showed no signs of melting.

Subsequent analysis confirmed that the high-temperature reaction had created a ceramiclike crust with exceptional thermal insulation properties. The material had not only passed the test but exceeded expectations by a wide margin.

Reflecting on the journey, I recognize that persistence, curiosity, and a willingness to learn from failure were crucial to this success. Although the company considered patenting the formulation, they ultimately opted to keep it a trade secret due to the complexity of the formula and process, believing it would be difficult for competitors to replicate. While I agreed with the decision from a strategic standpoint, I personally felt the loss of what could have been my first patent.

The innovation's potential extended beyond its original application. At one point, we even contacted the National Aeronautics and Space Administration (NASA) regarding its use in space shuttle heat shielding—especially after reports emerged of tile failures during atmospheric reentry. Unfortunately, the Challenger disaster halted all discussions as the shuttle program was suspended.

Nevertheless, I still consider this my most significant technical achievement. The original test sample remains in my office to this day—a constant reminder of the value of perseverance.

Methodical Approach and Lessons for Future Inventors

This breakthrough was not the result of a single flash of inspiration, but of a disciplined, step-by-step process. I began by carefully defining the performance requirement, then explored a wide range of material options, recording every failure as a source of new insight. Each unsuccessful test narrowed the possibilities and sharpened my understanding of the chemistry at play. By systematically altering ingredient ratios and controlling process parameters, I transformed a seemingly impossible challenge into a material that surpassed every expectation. For future inventors, the lesson is clear: innovation rewards those who combine relentless experimentation with careful observation, data-driven reasoning, and the courage to question assumptions. Creativity is not merely

> Creativity is not merely about bold ideas; it is about the patience to iterate, the humility to learn from failure, and the confidence to keep testing until the impossible becomes possible.

about bold ideas; it is about the patience to iterate, the humility to learn from failure, and the confidence to keep testing until the impossible becomes possible.

A New Move

Around this time, my wife Mary (a psychiatrist), our daughter Charlene, and our newborn Crystal had settled in New Jersey. We had just purchased a home when news came that our company had been acquired by a larger firm that planned to shut down operations in New Jersey and relocate to Massachusetts.

I was offered one of seven positions that were being transferred out of a total of 150 employees. While flattered, I was reluctant to move due to Mary's thriving private practice. The company president encouraged me to reconsider the matter and even offered his help to find Mary a hospital position through his connections. Though touched by the gesture, after careful discussion, we declined the offer and decided to pursue opportunities closer to home.

I sent my résumé to a local recruiter and, within a week, received a call from Sealed Air Corporation, a nearby company I had never heard of at the time. I assumed it had something to do with air conditioning. During the interview, I discovered it was the inventor of *Bubble Wrap®*, a product I had always found fascinating.

Two vice presidents (VPs) conducted an in-depth interview and expressed their great approval of my background. A final interview was scheduled with the VP of manufacturing, but he was unavailable. Days later, I received a call informing me that the company had decided to offer me the position based on the earlier interviews.

Ironically, I later learned that the VP of manufacturing, who had not interviewed me, was a strong advocate for a specific new polymer resin with which I had no experience. Had he interviewed me, I might not have received the job offer.

Sealed Air was significantly larger than my previous employers. I had my own office with a window, a lab technician, and access to a well-equipped laboratory. On my first day, a gentleman dropped by to welcome me. We had a long, friendly chat. After he left, my secretary informed me—with great amusement—that the man was the company's CEO. He had personally researched my background before our meeting.

Applying Knowledge and Embracing Innovation

My first assignment was to incorporate the new polymer resin—championed by the VP of manufacturing—into the Bubble Wrap formula. The material was relatively new to the industry, and few companies had the experience of processing it. Our initial trials failed, but each failure yielded insights. We eventually discovered that blending the new resin with other materials significantly improved processing. After six months of research and optimization, we successfully commercialized the revised product.

Unfortunately, due to overlapping patents, we could not obtain intellectual property protection. Still, the technical accomplishment was recognized internally, and I received a personal call from the CEO congratulating me.

Avoiding Tunnel Vision: A Lesson in Creative Thinking

While working on the new formula, I was also assigned to resolve issues with a newly introduced flame-retardant Bubble Wrap. Customers reported a powdery residue leaching from the material and contaminating their products. Our analysis revealed that one of the flame-retardant ingredients was incompatible with the polymer matrix, especially at elevated temperatures.

Despite exhaustive efforts using conventional ingredients and ratios, we found no improvement. I decided to take a different approach, experimenting with non-traditional additives. One unexpected combination eliminated the residue issue entirely—even under high heat. Extensive testing confirmed the new formula's stability.

This breakthrough led to the filing and eventual granting of my first patent: *Flame-Retardant Bubble Wrap*.

This experience reinforced a powerful principle: true innovation often requires stepping outside established boundaries. By resisting the urge to repeatedly refine conventional formulas and instead, exploring unconventional additives, I discovered a solution that not only solved the problem but also delivered a patentable breakthrough. The lesson for future inventors is clear—avoid tunnel vision. When a problem persists despite repeated efforts, pause, question assumptions, and deliberately explore alternatives that may initially seem unrelated or unlikely. Creative thinking is not merely about technical skill; it is the willingness to embrace uncertainty, challenge norms, and trust the process of experimentation. This mindset, once learned, becomes a lifelong tool for turning persistent obstacles into transformative opportunities.

Seeing the Bigger Picture

Innovation often begins with stepping back and viewing the problem through a broader lens. Our company previously manufactured absorbent pads for meat trays—used to capture purge during packaging, storage, and display. The primary challenge was to improve absorption and fluid retention, particularly under the weight of heavy meat.

Despite extensive experimentation, we could not achieve a solution that met our performance criteria. It became evident that simply increasing absorption in the pad resulted in leakage when pressure was applied. The project reached a deadlock.

At that point, we reassessed the problem from the customer's perspective. Instead of focusing solely on improving the pad, we asked ourselves: what if we could eliminate the pad altogether? Could the tray itself serve as the absorbent element? This redefinition of the problem opened new possibilities and inspired a different line of thought, one I set aside to explore further.

Inspiration in the Most Unexpected Place

Days later, we hosted a birthday party for my daughter Charlene's fifth birthday. As a magician entertained the children, one particular trick captured my imagination. He poured milk into a black bottle, and when my daughter attempted to pour it back out, nothing emerged. The milk had seemingly vanished.

Driven by curiosity, I examined the mechanics of the trick. After some trial and error, I discovered that a funnel inside the bottle directed the milk to the bottom chamber, effectively trapping it even when the bottle was inverted. This sparked an immediate connection to our earlier problem. What if we could use this same principle—fluid flowing into a hidden space where it couldn't escape?

Transforming the Concept into a Product

With this idea in mind, I visualized a meat tray with a funnel-shaped hole in the center. I nested a second tray beneath it and sealed the two trays together at the edges. Water poured into the top tray would flow through the hole and become trapped between the trays. When inverted or shaken, the water remained secure. It was a promising breakthrough.

To improve flow, I introduced channels and adjusted the slope of the top tray. Once the prototype was refined, I documented the invention in my monthly report. A few days later, I received the report back with a comment in green ink—used exclusively by our CEO: *"Excellent! Please call me when you get a chance regarding this new invention."*

He requested that I present the concept to the Board of Directors. Although nervous—this was my first board meeting—I prepared samples and overhead slides (this was before the days of laptops). The presentation was well received.

One board member, coincidentally the original inventor of the absorbent pad, joked after my presentation that my invention would render his obsolete. With good humor, he congratulated me, shook my hand, and encouraged me to continue the great work. The CEO assured me of full support from the board to pursue this project.

From Idea to Patent: And a Disappointment

With that support, I worked tirelessly on refining the concept and preparing a patent application. After two years, we received preliminary approval that the patent would be granted. However, just a month later, we were blindsided by a letter from the patent office: a similar patent had been granted in the Netherlands just three months earlier.

Neither our legal team nor the initial patent search had uncovered this prior art. The disappointment was profound. Still, it was a powerful reminder of the global nature of innovation—brilliant minds often arrive at similar solutions independently.

Creative Problem-solving Through Observation

Around the same time, I continued to explore ways to improve the performance of the absorbent pads. One day, while changing my baby daughter Crystal's diaper, I noticed how the diaper, despite being fully saturated overnight, did not leak. Cutting it open, I found a thick gel inside.

Further investigation revealed that the material was a *super absorbent polymer* (SAP), capable of absorbing up to 1,000 times its weight in water and retaining it in gel form. I immediately saw the potential application in meat pads.

However, adapting SAP to meat pads was not straightforward. The chemical composition of meat purge differed significantly from urine, and the absorption efficiency dropped. Through continued experimentation, we identified the optimal SAP particle size and redesigned the pad and machinery to incorporate it.

The final hurdle was approval from the Food and Drug Administration (FDA), as SAP was not previously approved for food contact. The regulatory process took over six years. Eventually, the SAP-based pad was commercialized, but unfortunately, our patent application was rejected due to similarities with diaper technology. It was a sobering lesson in how stringent patent offices can be with prior art.

Nevertheless, I continued enhancing the pad's performance, especially its absorption under load. These efforts resulted in three additional US patents for various design improvements.

Expanding Product Utility Through Innovation

While optimizing the absorbent pad, we also sought to expand its applications. Growth in raw meat packaging was limited, so we explored opportunities in other food-related areas—such as bacon cooking, which generates substantial grease.

The existing pad couldn't withstand cooking temperatures and required compliance with FDA standards. We sourced a high-temperature film, but sealing it without any adhesive was a challenge. Eventually, we found a film modified for heat-sealing. Using this material and sealing method, we developed and commercialized a cooking-compatible absorbent pad, which earned us another US patent.

Development was not without obstacles, but persistence paid off. The key lesson: when faced with barriers, stay the course.

Meeting Customer Needs

One of the most fulfilling projects I worked on was in response to the AIDS crisis, when concerns arose around the safe handling of biological specimens. There were numerous reports of fluid leakage during shipping, leading to contamination and safety risks.

Leveraging our knowledge from meat packaging, I redesigned the absorbent pad and enclosed it within a leak-proof bag. The new product featured a permeable inner film, a rugged outer film, and an absorbent core. Additional features included disinfectant-embedded absorbents, insulation against temperature extremes, and shock-absorbing properties.

The final product exceeded customer expectations and was granted a US patent. This was a textbook case of customer-centric innovation. Our marketing team identified the need, while R&D anticipated the problems and proactively developed solutions. By putting ourselves in the customers' shoes, we delivered true value.

The Inventor's Mindset

Value-added thinking is the foundation of invention. Instead of doing only what is requested, ask what *more* the customer might need—durability, convenience, safety, sustainability, or new use cases. These questions often lead to the next invention.

Creativity is often triggered by unrelated events—a child's birthday party, a diaper change, a magic trick. The brain constantly searches for connections. When a new experience resonates with a lingering problem, it can unlock unexpected solutions.

Invention thrives on curiosity, persistence, and the willingness to think beyond the obvious. Whether solving technical challenges, meeting regulatory requirements, or anticipating market needs, the path to invention is rarely linear—but always rewarding for those willing to walk it.

Research-driven Invention

During a public health crisis related to infectious diseases, I began considering potential solutions to address contamination during first-aid and medical procedures. I observed that while medical professionals always use gloves, such protective gear may not be readily available in households or informal settings. One particular issue caught my attention—people using cotton balls to wipe blood from body surfaces. This presented a clear opportunity to develop a simple, practical solution that could prevent contamination in everyday environments.

With these issues in mind, I developed a product called the *Blood Wipe Pad*. The design featured a flat absorbent surface bonded to a thick backing film, which served as a barrier to contamination. Additionally, the backing film was connected to a handle for safe and convenient handling. The product proved effective, and our company filed a patent application. A year later, the patent was granted.

Subsequently, I visited a potential client along with our marketing team. Although the customers were impressed with the product, they specialized in sourcing from established medical supply vendors and were not open to purchasing from a company with no prior experience in medical products. Despite obtaining a patent, the product was never commercialized for various reasons, including our company's lack of industry presence and marketing infrastructure in the medical space.

This experience exemplifies the nature of *research-driven invention*. I pursued this product based purely on a technical insight, without collaboration or validation from the sales and marketing departments. At the time, I had no understanding of the product's market potential or available distribution channels. This taught me a vital lesson: no matter how innovative your idea is, its success ultimately depends on marketability. Product development and commercialization are interdependent processes. In an industrial setting, thorough market analysis—including an assessment of market size, competition, and distribution—is essential before pursuing development.

For independent inventors, the situation may be different. They may focus solely on developing the invention and later approach specialized companies that can bring it to market.

Market-driven Invention

In many cases, invention originates from market demand. Customers may present problems requiring solutions. The sales and marketing teams evaluate such needs based on market potential, company capabilities, return on investment, and availability of R&D resources. Only if the opportunity aligns with strategic goals is the project approved—creating a valuable opportunity for the inventor to contribute.

One such opportunity arose during the anthrax contamination crisis in the US Postal Service. Our company was tasked with developing a solution to protect postal workers. I led a dedicated team to brainstorm and design solutions. One of my concepts involved a specially designed liner bag that could be placed inside mailboxes to prevent the spread of contamination.

While finalizing the design, I needed the dimensions of a standard mailbox. Rather than wait until the next day, I went to a nearby street and began taking measurements. As I was doing so, a police car approached. Given the sensitivity of the anthrax situation and the ongoing investigation, I realized how suspicious my actions might appear. I quickly put away my measuring tools and walked away. Fortunately, the officer did not stop, but it was a tense moment nonetheless.

Within a short timeframe, our team developed and reviewed multiple design concepts. Two designs—both mine—were selected as finalists. Patent applications were filed for both, and two years later, patents were granted. Although the products were never commercialized due to the resolution of the crisis, we took pride in our rapid and effective response to a national emergency.

This experience reaffirmed a critical trait for inventors: the ability to confront challenges and deliver timely solutions. Confidence, adaptability, and a results-oriented mindset are essential for survival and success in any industry.

Invention Through Technology Integration

When I joined Sealed Air Corporation, the company had recently surpassed $100 million in sales. Its two flagship products were *Bubble Wrap* and *Instapak foam*. Bubble Wrap is manufactured by thermoforming film to create bubbles, which are then sealed with a flat film to trap air for cushioning. Instapak is an on-site foam packaging solution created by mixing two chemicals dispensed around products for protective cushioning.

Early in my tenure, I studied both technologies and began exploring ways to combine their strengths. Bubble Wrap, while flexible and easy to use, can be vulnerable to popping under heavy loads. Instapak, though durable, lacks flexibility and convenience. I envisioned a hybrid product that merged the flexibility of Bubble Wrap with the durability of Instapak by filling the air bubbles with foam.

However, at the time, the Bubble Wrap and Instapak divisions operated independently with minimal collaboration. I wasn't sure how to pursue this cross-functional idea. I eventually pitched the concept to the R&D VP, expecting a positive response. Instead, he laughed and pointed out, "*Air is free; foam costs money. Why replace free air with expensive foam?*" It was a fair point. I hadn't considered cost implications or whether there was a market demand for such a premium product. This experience highlighted the importance of conducting *market research* before initiating development.

Interestingly, about a decade later, the market evolved, and the company introduced a product similar to my original concept. Increased shipping needs and the demand for better cushioning made such a solution viable. Unbeknownst to them, the foam division essentially revived my original idea. Seeing this product commercialized years later was deeply satisfying—it validated my early vision and underscored the importance of forward-thinking innovation.

Invention doesn't always align with immediate market needs. Being ahead of your time is not a flaw—it's foresight. However, in industries driven by short-term market pressures, such visionary ideas may not gain traction until the market catches up.

Independent inventors are uniquely positioned to think long-term. They can develop forward-looking innovations and offer them to companies when the time is right—often at a lower cost and lower risk for the acquiring company.

Visionary Invention for the Future

Bubble Wrap® is produced by sealing a flat film to a thermoformed sheet, creating air-filled bubbles that provide cushioning protection. While effective, this design results in a bulky product that is costly to ship and demands significant storage space. In the early years of my career, however, these concerns were not urgent—fuel was inexpensive, warehouse space abundant, and competitive pressures minimal. From the company's perspective, the original process worked well and the product was highly profitable, so there was little incentive to change.

Yet, I foresaw a different future. I envisioned Bubble Wrap manufactured without pre-trapped air, shipped flat, and inflated only when needed at the customer's site. I developed prototypes with an innovative design: rows of sealable chambers interconnected by a central inflation channel. The concept was technically sound and promised to revolutionize packaging efficiency. However, the company rejected the idea multiple times over the next 15 years. The market simply was not ready for such a disruption.

Decades later, the conditions that once made the idea unnecessary—low shipping costs and minimal competition—had changed dramatically. Escalating transportation costs and increasing market competition forced the company to rethink its strategy. At that point, the same concept that had once seemed premature became essential. A cross-functional team spanning R&D, manufacturing, sales, and legal personnel refined the design, secured three patents, and successfully launched inflatable Bubble Wrap into the market.

This journey illustrates the essence of a *premature disruptive innovation*—a solution conceived long before the environment could support its adoption. The lesson is clear: even brilliant, disruptive ideas may remain dormant until market forces align. For independent inventors, this creates a delicate balance. Patenting early provides protection and a potential first-mover advantage, but it also starts the clock on the limited patent term, leaving less time to commercialize when the market finally catches up.

Premature Disruptive Innovation

A *premature disruptive innovation* is an idea or invention that has the potential to transform an industry but appears *before the market is ready*.

Key Characteristics:

- *Visionary Concept*: The invention challenges conventional practices and offers clear long-term advantages.
- *Market Misalignment*: At the time of introduction, costs, customer priorities, or infrastructure make adoption impractical.
- *Rejection and Dormancy*: Companies or investors often dismiss the idea, seeing no immediate need.
- *Future Realization*: As market forces change—rising costs, new technologies, or shifts in demand—the innovation suddenly becomes not only viable but essential.

Example: Inflatable Bubble Wrap was envisioned decades before it was launched. Initially unnecessary, it became a success once rising shipping costs and market pressures aligned with its value proposition.

Takeaway for Inventors

Being "too early" can be as challenging as being "too late." Balance vision with patience, and recognize that timing often determines whether a disruptive idea thrives or waits in obscurity.

Don't Discount What's Right in Front of You

Innovation often comes from reimagining existing products for new applications. For example, Bubble Wrap is typically secured around items using tape or stretch film. During a visit by customers, I observed the difficulty they faced in securing the wrap. I began thinking about alternatives, but no immediate solution came to mind.

A week later, while testing *shrink film*—a material that tightens around objects when heated—I had a realization. What if shrink film could be combined with Bubble Wrap to create a self-securing cushioning material?

The primary challenge was how to attach shrink film to Bubble Wrap. Adhesives were too expensive, and heat-sealing risked premature shrinkage. I studied the material properties and found a narrow temperature window where the Bubble Wrap could be softened and sealed without triggering the shrink response. We modified our equipment to maintain this precise range, successfully producing the first *Shrink Bubble Wrap*—a value-added product that secured itself with heat. A US patent was granted for this invention.

This experience reinforced a vital principle: *never give up when facing roadblocks*. Re-evaluate the situation, question assumptions, and explore unexpected angles. Often, the solution is right in front of you—waiting to be discovered.

Collaborating Across Divisions Through Brainstorming

I was frequently invited to participate in brainstorming sessions across various divisions, as my perspective often brought a fresh take on challenging projects. One such opportunity arose with our InstaPak division, which specializes in on-demand cushioning foam created by mixing two reactive chemicals. The project goal was to develop a small, hand-activated bag that could mix these chemicals on demand to produce foam.

The key challenge was engineering a sachet that could securely contain the chemicals in separate compartments without premature mixing, yet allow for intentional activation by hand pressure. During the session, I proposed creating a frangible seal by printing adhesive in a specific pattern, ensuring controlled rupture under pressure. This idea was selected as the most promising solution and ultimately led to a patented product. Today, this frangible seal remains a fundamental component of one of the division's most successful innovations.

Gaining Competitive Advantage by Identifying Weaknesses in Existing Products

The Bubble Wrap division, equipped with advanced plastic processing capabilities, had an interest in expanding into adjacent markets. One such opportunity involved producing plastic bags for supermarket produce—an area already served by multiple competitors. A rival company had recently introduced a compact roll of folded bags paired with a dispenser that released one bag at a time.

Upon evaluating their design, we identified several functional issues with both the roll and the dispenser. I was tasked with leading the effort to develop an improved solution. Recognizing that understanding the problem is crucial to solving it, we spent days observing shopper behavior in stores and listening to their feedback.

Customers were accustomed to full-width bags pulled from rolls using two hands—one to hold the roll and another to tear the bag. The competitor's compact design allowed single-handed use but introduced confusion, as some customers mistakenly discarded the folded bags, assuming they were too narrow. Using these insights, we developed three new roll and dispenser designs that addressed user needs. All three were patented and successfully commercialized within the same year.

This experience reinforced a key lesson: product features are only valuable if they address real customer needs. Early user feedback is essential to delivering the right solution.

Addressing Customer Concerns with Innovative Solutions

Shortly after the launch of our new produce bag system, supermarket customers raised concerns about theft—shoppers could easily remove the compact bag rolls from the dispensers and take them home. The bag roll had a plastic core extending an inch on either side, which fit into the dispenser's channel and allowed free vertical movement.

Seeking a tamper-resistant design, I recalled a lock-and-key mechanism I had seen in my office. Inspired by how the key could enter a lock and stay secured once turned, I designed a solution using notches on the core ends and corresponding tabs at the channel's entrance. When the roll was inserted and rotated to align the notches with the tabs, it dropped securely into place. The roll was free to rotate and dispense bags but could no longer be easily removed. This design was patented and successfully commercialized, significantly reducing theft.

This case illustrates how keeping a persistent problem in mind can lead to creative solutions inspired by everyday observations.

Leveraging Core Competencies to Enter New Markets

One strategic approach to business expansion is to apply existing core competencies to new, related markets. We identified an opportunity in manufacturing Drainage Boards—rigid panels with bubble-shaped protrusions used to prevent water infiltration in building foundations. These boards, placed against underground walls, channel water away via geotextile fabric and drainage pipes.

Given the structural similarity to Bubble Wrap, we explored using our plastic processing expertise to manufacture this product. Initial trials using our equipment were promising. However, market analysis revealed a key limitation: existing products failed under high soil pressure at deeper installations. Two approaches were considered—thicker panels or high-modulus polymers. The former was cost-prohibitive, and the latter lacked chemical resistance.

We ultimately created a multilayer laminated panel: a strong polymer core provided structural integrity, while an outer layer made from the original chemically resistant material ensured durability. By adjusting the proportions, we achieved a cost-effective, high-performance product. This design was patented and successfully commercialized.

This project highlights the value of integrating partial solutions—rather than discarding materials or ideas that don't fully meet requirements, combining their strengths often leads to the optimal design.

Innovation Through Acquired Technologies

Our company experienced rapid growth through strategic acquisitions, each bringing new products and technologies. These integrations frequently inspired new inventions, as fresh perspectives revealed untapped opportunities. When a newly acquired company specialized in tamper-evident cash bags, we encountered a range of evolving challenges.

One major issue involved theft through manipulation of the adhesive closure. Thieves used heat (for example, from hair dryers) to soften the adhesive, steal the contents, and reseal the bag without signs of tampering. In response, the company developed a heat-sensitive ink that displayed a "VOID" message upon heating.

As criminals adapted, new methods such as freezing the adhesive with compressed air emerged. We countered this with hidden printing beneath the adhesive that would appear when the flap was lifted—triggered by any manipulation, hot or cold. Another tactic involved licking the adhesive before sealing, weakening its bond.

We resolved this by applying an invisible ink that changed color when moistened, flagging compromised packages before they left the facility.

Tamper-evident technology became a core competency, extending into forensic evidence bags and secure packaging. This acquisition directly led to several patented inventions and new commercial opportunities, showcasing how fresh perspectives on inherited technologies can yield significant innovations.

Driving Invention Through Product Extensions

Successful products often lead to opportunities for invention through extension. Following the commercial success of Bubble Wrap for protective packaging, the R&D team explored non-packaging applications. One innovative idea was to use Bubble Wrap as a solar pool cover—trapping heat, reducing evaporation, and maintaining water temperature.

However, challenges quickly emerged. While Bubble Wrap in packaging is rarely exposed to sunlight, prolonged ultraviolet (UV) exposure in pools caused the material to degrade. The team addressed this by adding UV-absorbing additives to the polymer and redesigning the bubble shape to reduce trapped air, thus improving shipping efficiency.

The pool cover became a profitable product. Yet, despite extensive safety labelling and customer education, incidents involving children becoming trapped under covers led to lawsuits. In response, the company made the responsible decision to discontinue the product.

This case underscores the importance of proactively evaluating safety and liability risks, even when a product seems successful. Responsible invention requires looking beyond technical feasibility to consider real-world usage and human safety.

Modifying a Product for Alternative Applications

One notable example of product evolution was the introduction of the *Bubble Cushion Mailer*, an extension of the Bubble Wrap line. Traditionally, small items required protective wrapping before being placed in mailing envelopes to withstand the rigors of shipping. Recognizing this inefficiency, an individual at the company (prior to my tenure) envisioned integrating the cushioning material directly into the envelope, eliminating the need for a separate wrapping step. This innovation led to the creation of the first cushion mailer.

The concept continued to evolve. Someone realized that shaping the Bubble Wrap into a pouch would further streamline the packaging process, resulting in the introduction of the *bubble pouch*. Building on this, a paper film was laminated to the pouch's exterior, creating the *first cushion mailer* with multiple advantages: content privacy, a writable surface for addresses, and space for postage.

Subsequently, *plastic cushion mailers* were developed by replacing the outer paper with a writable plastic film. This change introduced two key improvements: waterproofing and enhanced recyclability due to the all-plastic composition.

Driven by consumer demands for more convenient, efficient solutions, the R&D team continued to develop new variants. Additional Bubble Wrap product extensions included anti-static bubbles for electronic packaging, flame-retardant variants for high-risk environments, colored bubbles for promotional uses, and laminated bubble structures for specialty applications such as insulation.

Enhancing Products for New Uses

Numerous proposals aimed to adapt Bubble Wrap for novel applications. One such idea involved infusing the bubbles with *fragrance and color*. With uncertain market potential, I undertook the project independently during personal time, with my supervisor's support.

My hypothesis was that fragrances embedded within the polymer matrix would be slowly released, maintaining scent over time. Furthermore, each bubble pop could emit a burst of fragrance, even after years of storage. I tested two scents—*strawberry and pine*—and developed formulations with corresponding colors.

The initial trial with strawberry scent filled the facility with a pleasant aroma, drawing positive attention. However, by the day's end, the strong lingering scent led to some complaints. The pine-scented green bubble sheet, tested the next day, was similarly well-executed.

Remarkably, *25 years later*, I tested one of the original samples and could still detect the fragrance—validating the concept's long-term viability.

Missed Opportunities from Premature Abandonment

Traditionally, Bubble Wrap was colored during the extrusion process, limiting it to a single-color output. I was intrigued by the *iridescent films* on the market and wanted to create a similar visual effect for Bubble Wrap. However, manufacturing such films proved costly and technically challenging, and the idea was initially abandoned.

Despite setbacks, I continued experimenting. I attempted to thermoform iridescent film into bubble shapes, but the process compromised the film's optical properties. One day, while comparing two bubble sheets, I accidentally placed one on top of an iridescent film. To my surprise, the entire sheet appeared iridescent through *simple optical reflection*. This discovery eliminated the need for expensive processes or equipment, demonstrating how persistence and observation can lead to unexpected breakthroughs.

The lesson from this discovery was that even when solutions seem elusive, keeping an idea alive in the background often leads to insight when least expected.

Recognizing Unintended Product Features

Often, a product has latent features that can be harnessed for entirely different applications. Years after the introduction of Bubble Wrap, a team member observed its *insulating potential* due to the air-trapped bubbles.

However, the low melting point of the plastic made it unsuitable for high-heat insulation. A breakthrough occurred when a colleague proposed *laminating aluminum foil* to the bubble sheet. This not only enhanced thermal resistance and added flame retardancy but also introduced reflective insulation properties. The result was a high-value insulation material derived from a commodity product.

This concept led to further innovation, such as *foil-insulated bags* for shipping temperature-sensitive goods. Variations using decorative foil extended the product's use to items like gift bags and purses.

Inventors with a creative mindset often see applications others overlook. Bubble Wrap has inspired hundreds of such ideas—how many more can you imagine?

Improvisation as a Path to Invention

One summer, my office—located at a sun-exposed corner of the building—became uncomfortably hot. Seeking a sustainable solution, I constructed a *solar-powered fan* to mount atop my computer monitor.

Using a solar panel, a small fan, and basic wiring, I created a cardboard cone to direct airflow. The panel was affixed to the sun-facing window. In about an hour, I had built an energy-efficient fan that provided direct cooling without relying on the building's electricity.

Though solar fans existed, this project exemplified how *improvisation and creativity* can solve immediate problems in environmentally friendly ways—and it earned admiration from co-workers.

From One Idea to the Next

This success led to another concept: *a solar-powered fan inside a hard hat*, designed for outdoor workers such as soldiers and construction crews. Using a lab hard hat, I mounted a fan on top and wired two solar panels to either side.

On a hot day, I tested the prototype in the parking lot. The fan worked, and I enjoyed a cooling breeze inside the helmet. Some amused co-workers witnessed the scene, but eventually recognized the practicality of the idea.

This experience reinforced the principle that *one invention often sparks others*. Focusing deeply on a problem can lead to more innovative—and sometimes even better—solutions.

Repurposing Product Features for Unrelated Applications

A customer once approached us with a need for a *floating chemical pouch* that would gradually dissolve and distribute its contents in water. Traditional water-soluble bags failed, as partial dissolution caused the pouch to sink rapidly.

We tested a *bubble pouch made of water-soluble polymers*, and the results were remarkable. The air-filled bubbles kept the pouch afloat initially. As the outer film slowly dissolved, bubbles released air gradually, allowing the pouch to *sink at a controlled rate* while dispersing chemicals. By adjusting the film's composition, we could fine-tune the distribution timing.

This was a completely *unexpected use* of Bubble Wrap technology, exemplifying how products can be repurposed in ways the original inventors could never have imagined.

An Invention's Launch is Only the Beginning

When *Al Fielding* and *Marc Chavannes* invented Bubble Wrap in the 1950s, their intent was to market it as *decorative wallpaper*. The idea failed to gain traction. Eventually, a perceptive salesperson recognized its potential as a *protective packaging material*, launching a new era for the product.

This story illustrates a crucial lesson: inventing a product is only the *first step*. Real success lies in *discovering and leveraging its full potential*. Since its inception, Bubble Wrap has been adapted for numerous applications—from pool covers to reflective insulation—while its original use as wallpaper faded into obscurity.

Cost Considerations in Invention

A key determinant of a product's success is *cost-effectiveness*. No matter how innovative, a product will struggle in the market if it is prohibitively expensive. To justify higher costs, inventors must deliver *value-added features* such as improved performance, convenience, longevity, or sustainability.

At one point, I worked on developing a *sustainable, low-cost paper cushion product*. Starting with basic brown paper, I experimented with folding, twisting, and crumpling. One configuration—a *twisted paper rope*—showed promise for creating lightweight, bulked cushioning.

After discovering that pulling the paper sideways created a continuous twisted structure, I developed a method to extract the paper from the *inner roll layer*, simplifying the process. However, the twisted paper tended to unwind, posing a durability challenge.

Rather than fixating on the problem, I *shifted perspective* and explored braiding two twisted papers, similar to making rope. This approach *locked the structure* and significantly enhanced the cushioning performance.

To scale production, I designed a simple machine with spinning paper containers attached to a panel rotated by an electric drill. This prototype, which cost under *$25*, was capable of producing *200 feet per minute* of braided paper cushion.

Invention isn't solely about technical creativity—it's also about *practical execution*. Cost-conscious innovation is especially critical when developing solutions in the *commodity market*.

Inventions to Improve Everyday Life

For years, my daily commute exposed me to direct sunlight during early morning and late afternoon hours, often causing temporary vision impairment. As a shorter driver, I found that the vehicle's standard sun visor lacked the flexibility to provide adequate coverage. I frequently had to contort myself or adjust the visor to its extreme limits, often to little effect. After enduring this frustration for years, I began conceptualizing a solution: a fully adjustable sun visor extension that could supplement the factory-installed visor.

My objective was to design a sun-blocking frame with full mobility—capable of vertical and horizontal adjustments—to shield the driver's eyes from sunlight in any direction. The first prototype consisted of a movable rectangular frame mounted on a vertical rod, allowing vertical motion and positional locking. This rod was attached to a collar, which in turn housed a curved horizontal rod. This arrangement enabled lateral movement of the frame. A hook mechanism allowed the unit to attach securely to any standard sun visor and to be easily removed and transferred between vehicles. I developed a working prototype and installed it in my vehicle for testing.

The results were highly encouraging. The frame adjusted smoothly and effectively blocked sunlight even during challenging angles, such as low evening sun or from the sides. The curved rod configuration also allowed the frame to extend forward, enhancing coverage. I later modified the frame to accept interchangeable semi-transparent colored panels, offering a sunglass-like filtering effect.

Despite the innovation, the product met internal resistance when presented to my company. As a non-core automotive accessory, it was deemed outside the scope of our business interests. Additionally, concerns were raised regarding potential product liability. This experience reinforced a critical lesson: inventing a product is only half the journey—bringing it to market requires alignment with a company's strategic and legal frameworks. Inventors must evaluate feasibility not only from a technical standpoint but also from commercial and risk perspectives.

Responding to Customer Challenges

During the early phase of my tenure, our company operated a small division that produced paper bags for food takeout services. A common customer complaint was the use of metal staples, which occasionally ended up in food upon opening the bags. Clients requested an alternative that would not introduce foreign materials and would not require them to change existing bag-handling procedures.

I explored numerous alternatives—tapes, adhesive flaps, rubber bands, and mechanical twists affixed to the bag. Many of these options proved functionally sound but introduced additional materials, which the client found unacceptable. The challenge intensified with the stipulation to maintain the bag's structural integrity without added components.

Through experimentation, I discovered that tearing the paper flap into an arrow-like shape, folding it back, and interlocking it with the original fold created a surprisingly secure closure—essentially mimicking the function of a staple without adding anything foreign. However, this solution required manual tearing and folding by the end user, which was impractical.

Inspired by this discovery, I designed a modified punch tool that could replicate the arrow-shaped cut. The idea was to create a partially severed arrow flap still attached at the base. When pulled back, the arrowhead naturally folded and locked into place. I adapted an existing punch tool to test the concept and found that the arrow flap would engage and secure the closure automatically. The interaction between the tool's die and the paper strip introduced an unanticipated but welcome element of mechanical folding—serendipity playing a vital role.

I had a prototype punch manufactured by a local tool-and-die specialist, and the final product met all customer expectations. It eliminated metal staples, avoided the need for additional materials, and maintained existing workflows—resulting in increased customer satisfaction and fewer consumer complaints.

This experience underscored the importance of perseverance and creative problem-solving. Innovation is often incremental, and success can hinge on embracing unexpected insights. Meeting customer needs not only fosters long-term business relationships but also drives meaningful innovation.

Exploring Special Applications

During the Halloween season, our team developed a novelty product: glow-in-the-dark bubbles. By experimenting with phosphorescent chemical additives, we succeeded in incorporating luminescent agents into the polymer solution used for bubbles.

This innovation was intended for use in children's costumes to enhance nighttime visibility and safety, and it also opened the door to themed decorations.

While technically successful, the product's seasonality and low market demand limited its commercial viability. This illustrated a key principle: special-request or niche products may serve creative or safety functions, but the return on investment for research and development must be carefully considered when dealing with low-volume markets.

Applying Observed Technologies in New Ways

While on vacation in China, I encountered an intriguing toy—flat plastic pouches that inflated into animal shapes when struck. Curious, I dissected one and discovered a small pouch of vinegar surrounded by baking soda. Activating the toy involved breaking the inner pouch, triggering a chemical reaction that produced gas and inflated the outer chamber. Recognizing the potential of this principle, I saw an opportunity to develop an "on-demand" cushioning product.

I designed a prototype for flat bubble wrap, incorporating miniature chemical pouches within each bubble. When passed through compression rollers, the pouches would rupture, triggering inflation. This allowed the product to be shipped flat and inflated only when needed by the end user.

Although functionally sound, the product failed commercially due to several issues: high manufacturing costs, labor-intensive assembly, and concerns about chemical contamination. Despite its lack of market success, the project provided valuable insights into novel packaging mechanisms and opened potential avenues for future applications of chemical expansion.

Process Inventions and Trade Secrets

While product inventions are frequently patented, process innovations are often protected as trade secrets. Unlike product patents, which are publicly disclosed and enforceable, process patents are more difficult to monitor for infringement. For this reason, many companies choose to withhold public disclosure and instead maintain proprietary processes internally.

Over the course of my career, I developed numerous manufacturing process improvements. In many cases, we opted not to patent these methods but instead safeguarded them as confidential trade secrets. A more detailed discussion of patents and trade secrets is included later in this book.

A Fulfilling Career

I had the privilege of working for Sealed Air Corporation for 34 years, a tenure marked by passion and innovation. I often found myself thinking about work challenges even during vacations, and surprisingly, many of my best ideas emerged during those moments of mental reprieve.

I enjoyed strong relationships with the company's first two CEOs—Dermot Dunphy and Bill Hickey. Dermot, known for his green ink memos, regularly engaged with me on projects and offered unwavering support. I recall him once telling me, "*Charlie, what have you invented this month?*" His belief in my work provided both motivation and validation.

Bill Hickey, who succeeded Dermot, brought an engineering background and a keen interest in R&D. He actively collaborated with me on several projects and even co-authored a patent disclosure. His attentiveness extended beyond the workplace. During a trip to India, I was delayed due to a tsunami. Bill's immediate concern for my safety and his efforts to track my whereabouts were deeply appreciated.

Following Sealed Air's acquisition of a food packaging company, I transitioned into R&D for the newly formed division, which later led me to Corporate R&D. This broadened my exposure and allowed me to contribute to innovations across various sectors. In 2004, I was inducted into the Sealed Air "Inventors Hall of Fame" with 24 patents—a number that eventually grew to 86 by the time of my retirement in 2017. These include 38 U.S. and 48 international patents.

Even after retirement, I remain actively engaged in innovation, with 11 pending patent applications and over 300 invention disclosures documented. On the day I retired, I submitted two final invention disclosures—a fitting conclusion to a career devoted to creativity and problem-solving.

Final Reflections

Throughout my journey—from India to the US via Canada—my attitude toward invention has remained grounded in curiosity, problem-solving, collaboration, and a willingness to step beyond my comfort zone. These experiences shaped my career, guided my innovations, and strengthened my belief that invention is not confined to laboratories or workshops—it begins with a mindset and a keen eye for opportunity.

I've learned that technical knowledge alone does not lead to innovation. Equally important are persistence, creativity, open-mindedness, and the courage to pursue unconventional ideas. Innovation thrives when we refuse to give up, challenge conventional wisdom, and explore what lies beyond the obvious.

These are not just principles I followed—they are values I hope to pass on.

7

Capitalizing on Your Idea Through Entrepreneurship

Entrepreneurship is the process of identifying opportunities, establishing ventures to capitalize on them, and managing the associated risks. It involves initiative, vision, and the drive to bring new ideas to life—often with the aim of generating profit, creating value, or making a meaningful impact. Entrepreneurs are frequently motivated by the desire to develop something original or improve upon existing products, services, or systems.

At the foundation of entrepreneurship lie three core platforms: *Idea*, *Invention*, and *Innovation*. Although interrelated, each represents a distinct entry point for creating value and driving business success. Let us explore these platforms in greater detail.

The Power of an Idea

Successful entrepreneurial ventures often begin with a compelling idea. These ideas are frequently conceived by individuals with deep expertise or talent in a particular domain—be it communication, design, marketing, music, or technology. Leveraging their skills, such individuals are able to recognize unmet needs, develop targeted solutions, and launch businesses that deliver value to consumers.

What separates a profitable idea from a fleeting one is the entrepreneur's ability to identify a specific market demand, develop a compelling offering, and execute a business strategy effectively.

Examples of Idea-driven Entrepreneurship Include:

- *Oprah Winfrey* leveraged her communication skills to build a personal brand empire, starting with her talk show and later expanding into magazine publishing, television production, and her own network.
- *Reed Hastings* transformed the entertainment industry by shifting from DVD rentals to on-demand streaming, founding what is now the global giant, Netflix.
- *Melanie Perkins* co-founded *Canva*, making professional graphic design tools accessible to the average user through a simple, web-based platform.
- *Chichi Eburu* identified a gap in the beauty industry and founded *Juvia's Place*, a makeup brand designed specifically for darker skin tones.

These examples highlight how a strong idea, backed by expertise and execution, can lead to substantial entrepreneurial success.

From Necessity to Invention

The well-known adage, "Necessity is the mother of invention," reflects the human impulse to solve pressing problems. Inventors respond to challenges by creating new products, processes, or technologies. In previous chapters, we explored the invention process in detail, including ideation, solution development, prototyping, and intellectual property protection.

Inventors often play a transformative role in industry and society. Some notable examples include:

- Thomas Edison's invention of the incandescent light bulb, which brought affordable artificial lighting to the masses.
- Corning, the *American multinational technology company*, developed low-loss optical fiber, revolutionizing global communications.
- The creation of life-saving *vaccines*, such as the polio vaccine, which helped eradicate deadly diseases.

While not all inventions have such monumental impact, many smaller innovations significantly enhance convenience, safety, or quality of life.

Once an invention is created, the inventor faces critical decisions about how to commercialize and profit from it. Some may choose to:

- *License the invention* to an existing company for royalties.
- *Sell the invention outright* for a lump sum.
- *Build a business* around the invention, assuming both the risk and reward.

Licensing can be particularly attractive. A strong patent—similar to a well-equipped rental property—commands higher licensing fees if it features broad, enforceable claims that deter competition. Inventors may continue to innovate around the original concept, developing an evolving portfolio of patents that meet changing market needs.

However, not all inventors have the skills—or interest—to manage a business. In such cases, selling or licensing the invention is a perfectly valid and often profitable choice. For those with an entrepreneurial mindset, building a company around their invention may be a more rewarding path.

Innovation: Challenging the Status Quo

Innovation is the relentless pursuit of improvement and transformation. Innovators often venture into uncharted territory, identifying opportunities others overlook and taking calculated risks to introduce groundbreaking solutions.

While invention often arises from necessity, innovation can result in new needs and desires—suggesting that *"Innovation is the father of necessity"*. This perspective is exemplified by the evolution of technology. For example, the internet was not developed to fulfil a specific consumer need, but its existence gave rise to entirely new industries and expectations—ranging from online shopping and social networking to digital entertainment and cloud computing.

> Innovators often venture into uncharted territory, identifying opportunities others overlook and taking calculated risks to introduce groundbreaking solutions.

Examples of Disruptive Innovation Include:

- *Apple,* with products like the iPod and iPhone, redefined how we listen to music and interact with technology.
- *Uber,* by introducing ride-hailing via mobile apps, upended traditional taxi services.
- *Airbnb* leveraged the sharing economy to transform the hospitality industry.
- *Amazon* revolutionized retail with its e-commerce platform, logistics network, and cloud services.

Pursuing innovation as a business strategy can be risky and complex, but the potential rewards—market leadership, consumer loyalty, and transformative impact—can be immeasurable. Aspiring entrepreneur-inventors should recognize that support is available, from incubators and accelerators to angel investors and venture capital. Shows like *Shark Tank* provide a glimpse into both the excitement and the challenges of bringing innovations to market.

It's important to note that inventions and innovations are not always physical products. If your idea involves a *distinctive name, slogan, or logo,* consider *trademark protection.* If it involves *software, text, or creative content, copyrights* may be more appropriate. These protections strengthen your ability to defend your brand and capitalize on your creation.

Know Your Product's Potential

Before commercializing your invention, thoroughly evaluate its market potential. If it closely resembles existing products and lacks unique advantages, it may not be commercially viable—unless you can produce it at a significantly lower cost.

In some cases, a viable path may involve *selling the patent* to a manufacturer who sees value in eliminating a potential competitor. However, such deals may yield limited returns unless your invention offers compelling differentiation.

Selling an invention *without patent protection* is the least favorable approach. Without legal safeguards, you have no recourse if a negotiation fails or if your idea is misappropriated. If you must pursue this path, ensure that the potential buyer *signs an NDA* to prevent unauthorized use of your concept. Keep in mind that buyers may be hesitant to invest without any intellectual protection, as they would bear the cost and uncertainty of filing for a patent themselves.

Building a Strong Brand

A strong brand is a powerful asset that extends far beyond a logo or tagline. It encompasses the perceptions, emotions, and expectations associated with your company and its offerings.

A brand includes visual identity, stylistic elements, messaging tone, and customer experience—all of which contribute to your reputation and recognition in the marketplace.

The goals of effective branding are to:

- Differentiate your product or service from competitors.
- Establish trust and credibility with your target audience.
- Inspire customer loyalty and advocacy.

To build a compelling brand, begin by identifying your *target audience*. Conduct market research to understand their demographics, preferences, behaviors, and buying motivations. The clearer your understanding, the more precisely you can craft messages that resonate and build long-term relationships.

Study your *competitors* as well—identify their strengths, shortcomings, and market gaps. Position your brand to fill those voids and highlight your unique value proposition.

Once your brand is defined, *integrate it across all touchpoints*: product packaging, marketing materials, websites, customer service interactions, employee behavior, and even small details like your email signature. Consistency reinforces credibility.

Your *visual identity*—including your logo, color scheme, typography, and design elements—should be distinctive and reflective of your mission. A memorable logo can significantly boost brand recall and market presence.

If your brand includes a unique name, design, or slogan, consider *filing a trademark petition* to protect your identity and prevent imitation.

Protecting Your Invention

Securing intellectual property protection is a critical first step in monetizing your invention. Filing a patent application with the

USPTO is essential, though the process can be complex and often challenging. It is not uncommon for an application to be initially rejected. However, such rejections may be overcome through detailed responses and counterarguments. In some cases, patent claims may be granted, albeit in a limited form.

Inventors typically aim to secure patents with strong and broad claims to prevent competitors from circumventing their innovations. A patent with narrow or easily avoided claims may have limited commercial value. Potential licensees or buyers are unlikely to invest in weak intellectual property. Therefore, working closely with a qualified patent attorney to craft and negotiate broader, defensible claims is highly recommended. As previously discussed in an earlier chapter, strategic claim development is fundamental to creating valuable and enforceable patents.

It is equally important to recognize that holding a patent, in itself, does not generate revenue. The commercial value lies in how the patent is utilized—whether through production, licensing, or sale. Notably, even if the patent remains dormant, it retains legal power. If another party infringes upon it, the patent holder can pursue legal remedies and may be entitled to substantial damages, although litigation can be costly and complex.

Invention vs. Market Readiness

An invention with significant potential may still face challenges in commercialization if the market is not yet ready. Being ahead of technological or societal trends can lead to resistance, as industries may hesitate to disrupt the status quo. Often, the prevailing mindset is, *"Why introduce change when things are going well?"*

Disruptive inventions frequently require substantial investment and carry uncertain outcomes. In some instances, corporations purchase patents, not to commercialize them but to prevent others from doing so. Historically, examples include large automotive and oil companies acquiring electric vehicle patents while delaying development to protect existing business models.

A notable case within the Bubble Wrap industry involved the concept of inflatable Bubble Wrap—shipped flat and inflated on-site by customers. Although the idea addressed shipping and storage inefficiencies, it initially failed to gain traction because the market was thriving and customers were unconcerned with those costs. Only later, as oil prices rose and storage costs increased, did the innovation achieve commercial success, demonstrating the importance of timing in launching new products.

Licensing and Selling Your Invention

Many inventors choose to capitalize on their inventions through licensing or outright sale. This approach allows inventors to benefit financially without incurring the risks and expenses associated with manufacturing and distribution. While this path typically yields lower returns than starting a business, it is often quicker and more accessible.

Although it is possible to sell an invention without patent protection, holding a patent significantly strengthens negotiating power and perceived value. In some cases, inventors may license their patent to multiple companies and receive royalties from each. If your patented invention offers unique advantages over competing products, you are better positioned to command premium licensing fees.

Innovation Through Collaboration or Manufacturing

If you have established relationships with manufacturers, consider exploring collaborative opportunities beyond licensing. Working with them to further develop or refine your invention allows you to contribute as an innovator—someone who applies new ideas and improves upon existing ones to meet evolving consumer needs.

Alternatively, you may choose to venture into manufacturing and commercialization yourself. While this route offers the highest potential rewards, it also entails the greatest risks. Successful commercialization requires patent protection, market research, a solid business plan, adequate funding, and a strong brand and marketing strategy.

Some inventors, however, adopt a passive strategy, holding onto patents with the hope that others will infringe upon them, thereby creating an opportunity for litigation. While monetary awards from infringement lawsuits can be substantial, legal outcomes are uncertain and litigation costs can be prohibitive. Most disputes are resolved through settlements.

Invention, Innovation, and Entrepreneurship

Invention and innovation are distinct but interdependent concepts. An invention introduces something novel, while innovation involves applying that invention to create value. Entrepreneurship completes the trio, as it involves taking an invention or innovation and transforming it into a viable business.

An inventor becomes an entrepreneur when they take their creation to market, assuming both the risk and reward. Thomas Edison, for example, was a prolific inventor who also built enterprises around his innovations. Steve Jobs was both an inventor and a visionary innovator, famously transforming consumer technology. Though Jobs did not invent the iPhone himself, his leadership at Apple was instrumental in its development and success. Similarly, Elon Musk exemplifies the inventor-entrepreneur, in light of founding and leading companies such as Tesla, SpaceX, and Neuralink.

By contrast, many brilliant inventors, including some pioneers of the internet, focused solely on scientific progress without engaging in commercialization. Both paths are valid and necessary—one generates ideas, the other brings them to life in the marketplace

The Role and Power of Innovation

Innovation is more than creativity—it is the practical realization of ideas that solve problems or create new value. It spans a wide spectrum, including:

- *Technological Innovation*: Breakthroughs in products such as smartphones, autonomous vehicles, or cutting-edge software.
- *Process Innovation*: Enhancements in operational efficiency, cost reduction, and waste minimization, as seen in business process engineering.
- *Product and Service Innovation*: Introducing new offerings or improving existing ones to meet changing consumer needs.
- *Social Innovation*: Creative approaches to addressing societal challenges like poverty, inequality, and education.
- *Open Innovation*: Collaborative efforts across organizations and communities, embracing both internal and external ideas.

Innovation is essential for maintaining competitive advantage, driving economic growth, solving complex global issues, and improving the quality of life. It transcends technology, affecting economic, social, and environmental dimensions.

From Invention to Innovation

Although invention and innovation are separate, their integration is key. The inventor is often the idea generator, while the innovator is the visionary who transforms the idea into reality. Many inventors opt to sell their ideas to larger companies with the resources for commercialization. Others take the bolder step of building a business around their invention, becoming true entrepreneur-innovators.

Once an invention is launched, innovation becomes an ongoing process—refining, adapting, and enhancing the product based on user feedback and market evolution.

Understanding and Meeting Customer Needs

The foundation of business success lies in identifying and fulfilling customer needs. Launching a new product without deeply understanding your target audience can result in poor market reception, regardless of how innovative the product may be.

As markets evolve and competition intensifies, customer expectations become more complex. Companies must stay ahead of these shifts through proactive customer analysis, continuous product refinement, and strategic adaptation.

Success in today's dynamic market landscape hinges on your ability to remain agile, responsive, and customer-centric. Businesses that embrace innovation while remaining attuned to customer needs are best positioned for long-term growth and sustainability.

From Inventor to Innovator: Thinking Beyond the Prototype

Successfully capitalizing on an invention requires more than just a great idea—it demands a strategic, multifaceted approach. The path from concept to commercialization includes inventing the right product, securing robust intellectual property protection, understanding customer needs, manufacturing cost-effectively, and marketing strategically. Each of these steps is critical, and how they are handled can determine the ultimate success—or failure—of your entrepreneurial venture.

Innovation is rarely a one-time event. It is an ongoing process of refinement and adaptation to meet evolving consumer expectations. This requires the inventor to think like an innovator, possessing not only creativity but also the resilience and foresight to improve upon the original idea based on real-world feedback. Customer input will often reveal product shortcomings or suggest new features such as greater ease of use, enhanced safety, speed, compactness, or durability.

A fundamental pillar of innovation is identifying the right market. Misalignment between product and market can be detrimental. Consider the early history of Bubble Wrap: originally marketed as wallpaper, the product failed to resonate with consumers. However, repositioning it as a packaging solution led to its global success. This illustrates the importance of market analysis and the dangers of proceeding without it. Just as selling space heaters in a tropical climate or ice slabs in Alaska is unlikely to yield results, failing to align your product with the right audience can derail even the most promising invention.

For an inventor to transition into an innovator or entrepreneur, he/she must move beyond the comfort zone of ideation and embrace a broader vision. Not all inventors make this leap; only those who are willing to see their ideas through the lens of commercialization and customer value can evolve into true innovators.

Developing the Innovator's Mindset

An innovator must adopt a mindset grounded in openness, critical thinking, and problem-solving. It is important to be your own toughest critic—examining your invention not just for its potential, but for its weaknesses, market relevance, and usability. Rather than being driven by ego, let the focus remain on solving meaningful problems.

Innovation begins with communication and a willingness to challenge assumptions. You are no longer just an inventor; you are an active participant in product development. This requires thinking like a customer, marketer, business strategist, manufacturer, and even a legal advisor.

Think Like a Customer

Launching a product without a clear understanding of your target customers is a common pitfall. Even the most novel invention may fail if it does not meet a genuine need. Understanding customer needs is not merely beneficial—it is essential for commercial success.

Customer needs are typically centered on solving a problem or enhancing performance. Once these needs are clearly identified, your goal should be not just to meet, but to exceed expectations. Delivering value beyond expectations fosters customer satisfaction and builds long-term loyalty.

As markets evolve, so do customer expectations. Today's consumers are informed, discerning, and increasingly demanding. Staying competitive requires businesses to stay ahead of trends, monitor behavior, and adapt offerings accordingly. This means refining your product or service to align with changing preferences and continually striving to outperform competitors.

Convenience is a major driver of customer satisfaction. Whether it's online shopping, mobile payment systems, drive-through services, or 24/7 customer support, offering convenience can significantly enhance customer experience and differentiate your brand.

In addition, *customer experience* spans every touchpoint—browsing, purchasing, receiving support, and using the product. A seamless, positive experience builds trust, strengthens relationships, and turns first-time buyers into loyal advocates.

Pricing Strategically

Pricing is more than a financial decision; it reflects your understanding of customer psychology, perceived value, and market positioning. An effective pricing strategy should be informed by thorough research into customer behavior, competitor offerings, and cost structures.

Common pricing tactics include:

- *Psychological pricing*: Using prices like $99.99 instead of $100 to influence perception.
- *Bundling*: Offering products together at a reduced rate to increase perceived value.
- *Seasonal pricing*: Adjusting prices based on demand fluctuations throughout the year.

Developing pricing tiers can also help cater to diverse customer segments and maximize market reach. Always assess profitability, monitor market shifts, and adjust accordingly to remain competitive while meeting customer expectations.

Building Trust Through Reliability

Reliability is foundational for customer trust. Brands that consistently deliver high-quality products, fulfill promises, and respond promptly to issues position themselves as dependable and trustworthy. This reliability encourages repeat purchases and fosters long-term brand loyalty.

Proactively anticipating customer needs enhances satisfaction. By studying customer behavior, engaging in meaningful dialogue, and collecting feedback, businesses can offer tailored solutions—often before the customer even articulates the problem.

Sometimes, customers themselves may not fully understand their needs. They might misidentify the problem or seek the wrong solution. Innovators who truly understand their customers can guide them toward what they *actually* need, not just what they *think* they want.

Think Like an Innovator

Innovation thrives in a collaborative, supportive environment. No one brings a product to market alone. The process requires a team with expertise across design, engineering, manufacturing, marketing, and legal compliance.

As an innovator, foster a workplace culture that supports:

- *Open communication*: Create an atmosphere where team members feel safe sharing ideas.
- *Cross-functional collaboration*: Bring together diverse perspectives to spark new ideas.
- *Brainstorming sessions*: Regularly encourage the generation and sharing of new concepts.
- *Risk-taking*: Embrace experimentation and treat failure as a learning opportunity.
- *Empowerment*: Give employees autonomy and ownership over their ideas.
- *Support and resources*: Equip teams with the tools they need to innovate.
- *Recognition*: Celebrate not just results but the ideas that lead to them.

By cultivating these practices, organizations can transform into innovation hubs where ideas flourish and new products thrive.

Think Like a Marketer

While the development of a product often begins with identifying a gap in the market, long-term success hinges on what happens before the product launch. A key part of this process is *due diligence*—carefully evaluating the feasibility of the idea and understanding customer needs. Entrepreneurs must continually assess shifting market demands and position their solutions effectively.

Before launching a product, entrepreneurs must ask critical marketing questions:

- Who is the target market?
- How can we identify and engage with potential customers?
- What specific needs or pain points are we addressing?
- How do we align our product's value with customer expectations?
- How can we build trust and cultivate long-term customer relationships?

These questions help shape a focused marketing strategy that bridges product development with real customer demand.

Market Research and Feasibility

To answer these questions, businesses must conduct comprehensive customer research. This may involve:

- *Qualitative methods* such as interviews, focus groups, and observational studies.
- *Quantitative methods* such as surveys and controlled experiments.

This dual approach provides both depth and breadth, helping entrepreneurs to validate assumptions, avoid misinterpretation of feedback, and better tailor their offerings. Using multiple data sources strengthens insights and reduces the risk of drawing misleading conclusions from limited inputs.

Social media, straw polling friends or early adopters, and informal user testing are valuable starting points. Positive feedback can generate momentum; negative responses offer a chance to refine the product before significant investment.

Building a Marketing Strategy

Entrepreneurs must leverage both *online and offline marketing channels* to reach their audience and build awareness. Networking with industry professionals and potential partners can enhance visibility and access to resources. If the invention includes creative works—such as software, content, or media—copyright protection should also be considered as part of the go-to-market strategy.

Market analysis should extend beyond general interest—it should explore the *geographic, demographic,* and *psychographic* characteristics of the target audience. Many ventures fail due to misjudging demand or overestimating market readiness.

Customer research should uncover insights about what matters most to your target segment. Open-ended interviews, candid feedback sessions, and unbiased questioning reveal what customers truly value and what challenges they face.

From this research, entrepreneurs can build:

- A *value proposition*: a clear summary of the benefits your product delivers.
- A *unique selling proposition (USP)*: what differentiates your solution from competitors.

Even if the final product is not ready, a *prototype or Minimum Viable Product (MVP)* can demonstrate core features and elicit authentic user reactions. Testing how customers interact with your prototype helps you iterate and improve. This cycle continues until you achieve *product-market fit*—when your product effectively satisfies a substantial and profitable segment of the market.

Understanding and Evolving with Customer Needs

Effective marketing goes beyond initial interest—it requires understanding, evolving with, and adapting to customers' changing preferences. This involves:

- Personalizing interactions and customer experiences.
- Monitoring customer behavior through digital analytics, social media feedback, and direct engagement.
- Regularly updating offerings to maintain relevance.

A thorough understanding of customer "pain points" and motivations enables product refinement. Market needs shift quickly, so entrepreneurs must remain agile and responsive. Analyzing industry trends and being willing to pivot ensures sustained relevance.

Before engaging a customer, it's essential to understand their existing solutions, unmet needs, willingness to change, and growth ambitions. Avoid investing in ideas that lack genuine demand by validating hypotheses early through experimentation and data.

Competitive Analysis and Market Positioning

The presence of competitors often signals market potential rather than a barrier. By analyzing top-performing products, entrepreneurs can identify opportunities to offer superior value. Examine elements such as:

- Performance metrics and customer reviews.
- Product design and user experience.
- Traffic, pricing, and sales volume.

Even in saturated markets, differentiation in quality, user experience, or brand can create opportunities. Ensure your product addresses a real need better than existing alternatives.

Entrepreneurs passionate about their products—especially those that solve problems they themselves face—are often more persuasive and effective in promotion. Passion drives authenticity, which can influence others and attract attention.

Marketing strategies must answer essential questions:

- Does the product solve a meaningful problem?
- How much are customers willing to pay for a solution?
- Who exactly is the target audience?
- Is the addressable market large enough to justify investment?
- Who are the competitors, and how is your solution superior?

These answers guide the development of a compelling, differentiated offering.

Product Testing and Launch Readiness

Before a full launch, test your product with trusted users or early adopters. Real-world trials uncover usability issues and gather crucial feedback. Conduct structured interviews or usability testing to capture how users interact with the product in authentic settings.

Marketing and manufacturing teams must collaborate to produce functional models aligned with buyer expectations. This includes preparing:

- Product literature and sales collateral.
- Distributor and customer service training materials.
- Lead-generation campaigns, including trade shows, advertising, and direct marketing.

Involving the sales team early in the creation of marketing materials ensures buy-in and proper usage. Insufficient sales preparation is a common cause of failed launches.

Post-launch, ongoing support from engineering and customer service teams is vital. Prompt responses to customer feedback help retain early adopters and correct emerging issues.

Planning for Growth

After launch, focus shifts to scaling. Growth requires careful planning in the following areas:

- Staffing and personnel development.
- Equipment and infrastructure upgrades.
- Financial forecasting and balance sheet impact.
- Distribution, inventory, and warehousing logistics.

Anticipate challenges and refine your product based on recurring customer feedback. Continuous improvement keeps your offering ahead of evolving expectations.

Pricing Strategy

Pricing plays a central role in positioning and profitability. To develop a successful pricing model:

- Study competitive pricing and understand customer perceptions of value.
- Analyze your costs and set price tiers to accommodate different budget levels.
- Use discounts and promotions strategically.
- Maintain flexibility to adapt prices as the market evolves.

Effective pricing is more than assigning a number—it's about aligning with what customers value and how they perceive trade-offs. A well-informed, adaptable pricing strategy contributes to both customer satisfaction and business viability.

Think Like a Business Manager

Bringing a new product to market is a high-risk endeavor. Studies show that up to 90 percent of new product launches fail, often due to insufficient planning, poor differentiation, or a lack of alignment with market needs. To increase the likelihood of success, entrepreneurs must approach product development with the strategic mindset of a business manager.

Before committing resources, ask critical questions:

- Does this product, or a similar one, already exist?
- What differentiates your product from existing solutions?
- Who is your target customer, and what problem does your product solve for them?
- Why would customers choose your product over a competitor's?
- What are current customer opinions on existing solutions?
- How much are customers willing to pay for a better alternative?

Answering these questions provides essential insights to guide development, manage expectations, and ensure your product addresses a real market demand.

Each stage of your go-to-market strategy—from concept to production to launch—should be clearly mapped out with progress benchmarks. Establish measurable goals to track development, control timelines, and avoid ambiguity throughout the process.

Navigating Feature Prioritization and Expertise Gaps

During product development, teams may encounter challenges due to limited expertise, especially in areas involving technical or market knowledge. Prioritizing product features is crucial to ensure that your efforts align with user expectations, strategic goals, and resource constraints.

To manage this:

1. *Gather Extensive Data*: Engage with customers, stakeholders, and team members to identify what users truly value. This customer-centric approach ensures that decisions are based on validated needs rather than internal assumptions.
2. *Evaluate Impact*: Assess each feature's alignment with your product vision and its potential to drive user satisfaction or business value. Focus on high-impact functionalities over those with limited relevance.
3. *Use Prioritization Frameworks*: Apply tools such as the MoSCoW method (Must Have, Should Have, Could Have, Won't Have) to structure decision-making. These frameworks help objectively rank features and reduce the influence of knowledge gaps.
4. *Foster Cross-functional Collaboration*: Conduct brainstorming workshops and collaborative planning sessions to leverage

diverse perspectives. Inclusive input often uncovers innovative ideas and strengthens buy-in across departments.

5. *Iterate Continuously*: Feature prioritization is not static. As market dynamics evolve and customer feedback emerges, revisit and revise your roadmap accordingly.
6. *Align with Resource Constraints*: Be realistic about your team's capabilities. If certain features exceed current expertise, consider investing in training, hiring specialized talent, or simplifying development to align with available resources.

Budgeting for a Successful Launch

Effective budgeting is fundamental to the success of a new product launch. Your financial plan should align closely with strategic goals and cover all phases from development through distribution. Best practices for budgeting include:

- Defining clear objectives and project scope
- Estimating development, marketing, and operational costs
- Forecasting revenue and analyzing cash flow
- Aligning financial projections with broader business goals
- Collaborating with stakeholders to gain alignment
- Monitoring results and adjusting forecasts based on performance

A well-prepared budget serves as both a roadmap and a control mechanism, ensuring resource efficiency throughout the launch process.

Think Like a Manufacturer

Manufacturing plays a central role in product commercialization. Even the most promising innovations can falter if the transition from prototype to production is poorly managed. Therefore, once you've validated the market opportunity and refined your concept, shift your focus to executing a robust manufacturing strategy.

Planning and Prototyping

Begin by developing a *minimum viable product (MVP)* that meets essential customer needs. Collaborate with engineers, department heads, and technical experts to refine the product. Secure internal approvals, and if possible, engage trusted customers early for feedback.

Before initiating production, conduct a *risk analysis* to anticipate potential challenges and document them in a risk register. Simulate the production process during prototype testing to identify design flaws or process inefficiencies.

Core Elements of a Manufacturing Plan

- Define clear product specifications and engineering documentation
- Finalize all design details before moving to production
- Select appropriate materials and manufacturing methods
- Establish a timeline with resource allocations and budgets
- Identify and qualify reliable suppliers
- Conduct pilot runs to uncover unforeseen issues
- Implement quality assurance protocols at every stage

Once in production, *ongoing quality control* is essential. Post-production inspection ensures product integrity and safety. Establishing a strong link between engineering and manufacturing teams improves data consistency and accelerates time-to-market.

Working with Manufacturing Partners

If you plan to outsource manufacturing, choose your partners carefully. A valuable manufacturer should act as an extension of your team—offering expertise, guiding material selection, and helping optimize the production process.

Avoid viewing manufacturing merely as a transaction. A good partner can be instrumental in reducing costs, improving product quality, and navigating complex logistics.

Managing the Supply Chain

A resilient supply chain is critical. Delays, shortages, or compliance issues—such as sourcing from embargoed regions—can derail your launch. Conduct due diligence on all suppliers and distribution partners to minimize risks, especially if you intend to sell to government or regulated markets.

Preparing for Market Launch

Final preparations before a launch include:

- Securing inventory across all configurations and sizes
- Finalizing packaging—both from a functional and branding perspective
- Coordinating distribution and fulfillment logistics
- Gathering last-minute customer feedback to validate product performance

After the launch, maintain a responsive support system. Early adopters may raise issues that require quick fixes or product updates. Use this feedback loop to identify improvement opportunities and inform the development of next-generation products.

Think Like a Lawyer

Legal considerations are critical throughout the invention-to-commercialization lifecycle. Protecting your intellectual property early and effectively, safeguards your idea from infringement and strengthens your market position.

Protecting Your Idea

Begin with a *novelty search* to determine whether your idea is truly unique. Even if your own search yields no prior art, the patent office's review may reveal existing claims. Engage a qualified *patent attorney* early in the process to avoid investing in a product that cannot be protected.

Once your concept is sufficiently developed, work with your attorney to file a patent application. As the inventor, you bring critical technical insights that can help broaden the scope of the patent claims. A strong patent discourages competitors from making minor alterations to copy your idea.

Ongoing Legal Vigilance

After launching your product:

- Monitor the market for potential patent infringement
- Be prepared to take legal action against infringers if necessary
- Ensure that any product modifications do not infringe on existing patents
- Consider filing additional patents for improvements and variants

Protecting Process Inventions

If you've developed a proprietary process that is difficult to patent or enforce, consider *maintaining it as a trade secret*. This requires implementing strict confidentiality protocols internally and externally.

If a competitor files a patent that threatens your business, consult your legal team to assess its validity. If appropriate, you may be able to *challenge and invalidate* the patent.

Confidentiality Agreements

If you need customer feedback prior to filing a patent, always use an *NDA* to protect your idea. Sharing product details without an NDA can jeopardize your rights and potentially render your invention unpatentable.

Conclusion

Transforming a great idea into a successful business requires vision, strategic thinking, and persistence. Success depends not only on innovation but also on evaluating opportunities, protecting intellectual property, and building a strong brand. By approaching entrepreneurship through the lenses of a business manager, manufacturer, and lawyer, innovators can develop a well-rounded strategy.

Being a successful entrepreneur goes beyond invention—it involves understanding customer needs, building relationships, setting smart prices, and fostering ongoing innovation. Whether choosing to license, sell, or grow a business, success hinges on the ability to manage risk, seize opportunities, and execute effectively.

While entrepreneurship carries risk, with the right mindset and preparation, it offers the potential to turn creativity into meaningful and lasting value. Innovation thrives on collaboration, iteration, and adaptability—and those who embrace this process can turn ideas into impactful enterprises.

8

The Entrepreneur

An entrepreneur is an individual who initiates, organizes, and operates a business venture—typically one that introduces a product or service to the market. Entrepreneurs are often innovators, transforming ideas into tangible offerings and assuming the financial and operational risks associated with their endeavors. In return, they stand to reap the rewards of success, both monetary and reputational.

Entrepreneurship is the art and discipline of identifying market opportunities and creating ventures to address them. Entrepreneurs aim to meet consumer demand while generating profit, often disrupting traditional business models through innovation. Their contributions are vital to economic development, job creation, and technological progress.

Traits of a Successful Entrepreneur

Entrepreneurs are typically characterized by high motivation, passion, and persistence. They demonstrate resilience in the face of setbacks and possess the leadership skills needed to manage teams, inspire others, and execute their vision. Adaptability, strategic thinking, and a keen understanding of market dynamics are critical to success in a rapidly changing business environment.

Entrepreneurs are typically characterized by high motivation, passion, and persistence. They demonstrate resilience in the face of setbacks and possess the leadership skills needed to manage teams, inspire others, and execute their vision.

To scale a startup effectively, entrepreneurs must focus on sound operations, customer-centered culture, targeted marketing, and strategic partnerships. Leveraging technology and embracing innovation can enhance efficiency and establish a competitive edge. Continuous learning and responsiveness to market feedback are essential for long-term growth and scalability.

Can Anyone Become an Entrepreneur?

Yes—entrepreneurship is open to anyone. While some individuals may have a natural aptitude for it, entrepreneurial skills can also be developed through education, experience, and mentorship. There are no specific prerequisites in terms of education, background, or demographics. The key is possessing the drive to take initiatives, solve problems, and adapt to challenges.

An entrepreneurial mindset—marked by proactivity, creativity, and outcome-oriented thinking—can be cultivated over time. However, success varies widely. According to Zippia, the online site for people seeking jobs, approximately 22 percent of small businesses fail within the first year, 50 percent within five years, and nearly 66 percent within a decade. A willingness to learn, persist, and evolve is essential.

Business Owner vs. Entrepreneur

While the terms "business owner" and "entrepreneur" are often used interchangeably, they reflect different approaches.

- A *business owner* typically focuses on maintaining and optimizing an existing business. They aim for stability, profitability, and sustainable operations. Examples include restaurateurs or retail store operators who emphasize consistent service and operational efficiency.
- An *entrepreneur*, by contrast, seeks to launch new ventures, often involving innovative or disruptive ideas. They embrace higher levels of risk and uncertainty, pursuing rapid growth and change. Examples include tech startup founders or pioneers of entirely new industries.

Types of Entrepreneurs

Entrepreneurs come in many forms. Four common archetypes include:

- *The Inventor*: Visionaries who create entirely new products or services.
- *The Small Business Owner*: Individuals operating local businesses, such as consultancies or family-owned stores.
- *The Online Entrepreneur*: Digital business creators using the internet to market and sell goods or services, including bloggers, e-commerce vendors, or software developers.
- *The Home-based Business Owner*: Entrepreneurs who operate from home, such as artisans or small service providers.

Characteristics of Successful Entrepreneurs

Successful entrepreneurs often juggle multiple roles, such as innovators, marketers, accountants, product developers, and strategists. Many operate as one-person teams in the early stages, making every critical decision themselves. This requires broad competence across various business functions and the capacity to learn rapidly.

They are competitive by nature, driven to succeed and overcome challenges. Some grow their ventures into thriving enterprises or exit through acquisition. Importantly, successful entrepreneurs recognize that they cannot succeed alone. Building strong networks—of mentors, partners, investors, and collaborators—is crucial.

Entrepreneurs are made, not born. With the right training, support, and perseverance, anyone can develop the competencies needed to thrive. While ideas are essential, execution, adaptability, and access to resources such as funding are equally critical. Those who balance creativity with practicality are better positioned to bring their ideas to life.

Starting a Business

Entrepreneurs do not merely leap into action. They begin by validating demands, confirming that customers value the proposed solution, and assessing production feasibility. In the process, they often refine or pivot their original ideas.

While some inventors choose to license or sell their creations to established firms, others opt to build businesses around them. The latter path demands resourcefulness, as entrepreneurs must learn the commercialization process, secure funding, and build necessary capabilities from the ground up to the top level.

It's not advisable to start a business simply for the sake of ownership. Instead, identify a problem worth solving. If others share the same need and are willing to pay for your solution, you have a foundation. Scale that solution thoughtfully—from a freelance offering to a small business, and possibly to a full-scale enterprise.

Starting small—while retaining a day job, for example—can reduce financial pressure. A detailed business plan is essential, outlining the target market, cost structure, customer acquisition strategy, and value proposition.

Entrepreneurial Readiness

Success hinges not only on a good idea but also on personal readiness. Entrepreneurs must understand why they are starting their venture, be open to experimentation, and possess a well-honed leadership style. If you cannot articulate your purpose, your chances of sustaining the effort required are slim.

Key skills to develop include:

- *Adaptability*: Responding flexibly to feedback and market shifts.
- *Resilience*: Recovering from setbacks and turning failure into learning.
- *Communication*: Articulating your vision and influencing stakeholders.
- *Leadership*: Inspiring and managing others effectively.
- *Problem-solving*: Identifying obstacles and implementing solutions.

Before launching, test your concept with a trusted group, review market research, and stay informed on industry trends. Establish performance metrics and be prepared to adjust course if needed.

While no formula guarantees success, cultivating these attributes increases your chances. Entrepreneurship involves calculated risks and continuous learning—but for those with a compelling vision and the tenacity to pursue it, the rewards can be transformative.

Skills and Traits

Becoming an entrepreneur requires more than a great idea—it demands a distinct mindset and a set of refined traits that support initiative, resilience, and vision. The journey of entrepreneurship is often solitary in its early stages and fraught with challenges, requiring a unique blend of leadership, discipline, and adaptability. The following section outlines the critical qualities that contribute to entrepreneurial success.

Leadership

Entrepreneurship begins with leadership—of oneself, one's ideas, and eventually, one's team. Not everyone is suited for this path, and a self-assessment of your leadership capabilities is crucial. Can you guide yourself through uncertainty, long hours, and limited resources without external motivation? True leaders often emerge as the go-to person in group settings, are consulted for opinions or decisions, and have experience in supervisory or managerial roles.

Effective leadership requires strong communication, a compelling vision, and the ability to mobilize others toward a common goal. A good leader earns trust and respect by modeling positive behaviors, demonstrating confidence, and creating a work environment that fosters collaboration, integrity, and motivation.

Entrepreneurs embrace challenges and act as catalysts for change. They exhibit unwavering focus on their goals, remain solution-oriented under pressure, and persist even when faced with setbacks. Leadership also means adapting to changing markets, technologies, and consumer needs—seeing disruption not as a threat, but as an opportunity to innovate and improve.

Confidence and Risk Tolerance

Successful entrepreneurs exhibit high levels of confidence—in their abilities, their business model, and their long-term vision. Confidence is essential while building credibility with customers, investors, and team members.

Entrepreneurship inherently involves risk. However, successful entrepreneurs are not reckless; they are calculated risk-takers. They evaluate the potential downsides, assess the likelihood of worst-case scenarios, and develop contingency plans. They understand that failure is not final but part of the learning process. This mindset allows them to move forward boldly, even in the face of uncertainty.

The willingness to take risks often stems from a deep belief in one's mission. Rather than asking, "*Will this work?*" entrepreneurs ask, "*What's the worst that could happen?*" and, "*Can I handle that outcome?*" If the answers are manageable, they proceed with courage.

Optimism and Resilience

Optimism fuels entrepreneurial perseverance. It's the belief that, despite obstacles, success is possible. Optimism encourages risk-taking, inspires confidence, and enhances decision-making, even when the outcomes are uncertain.

Entrepreneurs train their mindset to view failure as a feedback and persist through adversity. They don't dwell on setbacks but seek to understand what went wrong and how to improve. Resilience and optimism go hand in hand—together they provide the emotional strength to keep moving forward.

Curiosity and Problem-solving

At the heart of entrepreneurship is curiosity—the desire to understand how things work, ask questions, and explore alternatives. Successful entrepreneurs are lifelong learners who actively seek knowledge, investigate trends, and stay open to new perspectives.

Problem-solving is a core entrepreneurial skill. Entrepreneurs identify problems and innovate practical solutions. They are willing to admit when something doesn't work and pivot their approach when needed. They also understand that they don't have all the answers, which is why they surround themselves with advisors, mentors, and experts who can provide valuable insights.

Passion and Persistence

Passion is the driving force behind sustained entrepreneurial effort. Entrepreneurs are deeply invested in their ventures because they believe in the value of their product or service. This intrinsic motivation goes beyond financial gain—it's rooted in purpose and fulfillment.

Passion fosters persistence. Even when progress is slow or obstacles appear insurmountable, passionate entrepreneurs continue pushing forward. Their belief in the impact of their work allows them to maintain momentum and inspire others to share in their vision.

Creativity and Innovation

Creativity is essential for developing unique solutions and differentiating a business in a crowded marketplace. Entrepreneurs often face resource constraints, which force them to think creatively and make the most of what they have.

Creative entrepreneurs not only generate ideas but also implement them effectively. They look at problems from multiple angles, test different strategies, and embrace innovation as a continuous process. Even those who don't naturally consider themselves creative can develop this skill by consistently exploring new ideas, evaluating alternatives, and seeking inspiration from diverse sources.

Interpersonal and Communication Skills

Entrepreneurs must communicate their vision clearly—to customers, partners, investors, and employees. Strong interpersonal skills enable them to build networks, form alliances, and foster trust.

They must also be persuasive, empathetic, and able to adapt their communication style to different audiences.

This ability to inspire and influence others is not innate to all entrepreneurs, but it can be cultivated. Practice, mentorship, and real-world experience play a significant role in developing these soft skills.

Willingness to Learn

The entrepreneurial journey is one of continuous learning. Successful entrepreneurs are humble enough to recognize that they don't know everything and are willing to learn from every interaction. Whether it's through formal education, industry research, or lessons learned from failure, they constantly seek to grow and strengthen their knowledge base.

They listen actively, ask insightful questions, and stay informed on trends, emerging technologies, and customer needs. Lifelong learning is a hallmark of effective entrepreneurship.

Opportunity Recognition and Strategic Thinking

Entrepreneurs are skilled at identifying unmet needs and turning them into business opportunities. They are observant and quick to connect patterns that others might miss. By maintaining an outward focus, they identify ways to enhance existing products, enter underserved markets, or create entirely new industries.

They also excel in strategic thinking—setting long-term goals, analyzing competitive landscapes, and adapting business plans based on performance data. This forward-thinking approach allows them to anticipate changes and make proactive decisions.

Thriving Amid Uncertainty

Uncertainty is inevitable in business, but successful entrepreneurs view it as an arena for growth. Rather than being paralyzed by ambiguity, they remain composed and focus on what they can control. They make contingency plans, manage risks, and stay aligned with their vision.

Entrepreneurs understand that setbacks are not failures but opportunities to correct the course they are on. They are comfortable in unstructured environments and often thrive where others falter.

Discipline and Work Ethic

Discipline is the foundation of sustained effort. Entrepreneurs often start their businesses while managing other responsibilities, requiring them to sacrifice personal time and energy. Self-discipline enables them to stay consistent even when motivation wanes.

However, discipline also involves balance. Entrepreneurs must avoid a burnout by managing time wisely and knowing when to delegate or step back. Long-term success is built on sustainable effort and healthy boundaries.

Adaptability and Flexibility

Markets evolve, consumer behavior shifts, and technologies advance. Successful entrepreneurs stay flexible and open to change. They test new ideas, iterate quickly, and let go of outdated practices when necessary.

Adaptability also includes being responsive to workforce dynamics. For instance, applying rigid, outdated management styles to modern teams may hinder growth. Agile entrepreneurs embrace change and create inclusive environments that attract top talent.

Hands-on Involvement

Even as their businesses grow, entrepreneurs often remain hands-on in operations. They maintain a deep understanding of how their business functions and ensure quality by staying engaged. This doesn't mean micromanagement—it encompasses knowing what's happening across departments and fostering strong relationships with team members.

Being hands-on reflects the entrepreneur's passion and commitment to excellence. It reinforces their role not only as a leader but as a contributor who values every aspect of their venture.

Habits of Successful Entrepreneurs

Entrepreneurs often surround themselves with mentors, participate in business communities, and actively seek feedbacks. They stay up to date on industry trends and emerging technologies and apply insights from their network to refine their strategies.

They focus on industries aligned with their interests and strengths and build specialized knowledge. Strategic business planning—including defining goals, understanding market needs, and tracking performance—is a constant process, not a one-time event.

They are also alert to differentiation opportunities, whether by targeting a unique niche, improving existing solutions, or developing disruptive innovations that redefine markets.

The Entrepreneurial Mindset

Successful entrepreneurs cultivate a mindset focused on innovation, adaptability, and resilience. This mindset is not merely a byproduct of ambition; it is a deliberate, disciplined approach to thinking and problem-solving. It goes beyond the oversimplified formula of *have an idea, secure funding, and start a business*. True entrepreneurial success demands the ability to navigate ambiguity, confront unexpected challenges, and maintain momentum in the face of setbacks.

While some individuals may naturally possess an entrepreneurial disposition, the mindset itself can be learned and developed. It requires a conscious effort to identify the knowledge gaps, seek relevant learning opportunities, and take calculated actions. Entrepreneurs must remain curious, open to feedback, and committed to continuous personal and professional growth.

One effective strategy is to adopt a "first principles" approach to problem-solving—a concept popularized by Elon Musk. Rather than reasoning by analogy or convention, "first principles" thinking involves breaking down complex problems to their fundamental truths and reasoning upward from there. This method encourages original solutions rather than relying on what has been done before.

Having a trusted mentor is invaluable in this journey. Mentors offer practical insights, guide strategic decisions, and connect entrepreneurs to influential networks. They can introduce you to potential collaborators, investors, or partners who might otherwise be difficult to access. Learning from those with real-world experience accelerates the development of the entrepreneurial mindset.

This mindset empowers you to identify problems and solve them using logical, foundational reasoning. It also sharpens your ability to define your target market, understand customer needs, approach challenges with curiosity, and persevere through adversity. An entrepreneur is deeply involved in every phase of the process—from concept to commercialization—and must understand each stage with clarity and purpose.

Business Acumen

A compelling idea is merely the starting point. To turn it into a successful venture, you must understand your deeper motivation for starting a business. Passion and purpose are critical, particularly when trends fade or obstacles arise. Select a business concept that genuinely excites you—something you're willing to commit to long-term.

Building a business requires more than enthusiasm. You need a sound business plan, a solid network, and essential entrepreneurial skills such as adaptability, resilience, and strategic thinking. Staying informed about industry developments, cultivating mentors, and maintaining a clear focus on your goals are equally important.

Start by identifying a product or service that aligns with your interests and fulfills a market need. Ask whether your potential customers will find value in what you're offering. Conduct thorough market research to understand customer pain points, analyze competition, and validate the feasibility of your business concept.

Subscribe to trade publications, follow market trends, and engage with professionals in your field. Attending networking events and joining online communities will not only enhance your knowledge but also expand your network. Building relationships with customers, suppliers, and investors is essential to your long-term success.

As your business grows, you'll need to collaborate with every department—sales, marketing, supply chain, finance, legal, and more. Each function plays a vital role in product success. Sales and marketing aim to deliver features that resonate with customers. The supply chain ensures scalability and manufacturability. Finance keeps the venture within budget. Legal teams secure intellectual property rights and confirm freedom to operate. The entrepreneur must remain engaged throughout these cross-functional processes.

Product Development vs. Product Management

Although often used interchangeably, product development and product management are distinct disciplines. Product development focuses on building the product—its engineering, design, and implementation. Product management involves overseeing that development process with a broader view of the product's lifecycle, market alignment, and strategic positioning.

A product manager leads the overall strategy and vision, bridging communication across departments. They initiate ideation, manage research, guide development, and oversee the launch. In contrast, product developers (such as engineers and designers) are tasked with creating and refining the product itself.

Product managers also collaborate with marketing and sales teams to develop go-to-market strategies and assess post-launch performance. Senior leadership typically provides final approval before a product moves to launch. Additional contributors—in fields such as finance, engineering, and legal—may play vital roles depending on the complexity of the product.

Product Development Team

The product development process is a multidisciplinary effort led by the product manager. They coordinate all phases from ideation to market launch, acting as a central hub for communication between stakeholders.

- *Project Managers* support cross-functional communication, track goals, and ensure task alignment.
- *Design Teams* contribute during prototyping to visualize the concept and enhance user experience.
- *Development Teams* bring the product to life—often through website integration or physical prototyping.
- *Marketing Teams* create and test campaign strategies and evaluate results after the launch of the product.
- *Sales Teams* align product features with market demand and report on performance metrics.
- *Senior Leadership* provides the final go-ahead for launch decisions.

Other departments—such as finance, engineering, and legal—play critical roles, particularly in compliance, budgeting, and risk management.

Product Development Plan

Creating a product development plan involves defining clear objectives, aligning stakeholders, and managing resources effectively. Begin by establishing measurable goals that reflect customer needs and market opportunities.

Develop a roadmap that outlines major stages, timelines, and required resources. This includes early ideation, concept testing, and strategic alignment. Monitor progress continuously, adapt to new information, and refine your approach based on feedback.

Stages of Development

1. *Idea Generation*: Brainstorming and gathering customer insights.
2. *Prototyping*: Creating visual or functional models to evaluate the concept.
3. *Feasibility Analysis*: Assessing technical, financial, and operational viability.
4. *Minimum Viable Product (MVP)*: Building a version with only core functionalities to test market response.
5. *Iterative Testing*: Refining the prototype through continuous feedback and stakeholder input.
6. *Design Finalization*: Collaborating with vendors, adjusting designs, and obtaining approvals.
7. *Validation and Testing*: Conducting final tests on functionality, usability, and marketing readiness.

Once all elements are validated, the product is ready for full production and launch.

A successful launch depends on seamless coordination, detailed planning, and agile execution. The development plan serves as your blueprint, helping you navigate complexities and bring your vision to life.

The Entrepreneur: Leading Your Business

Establishing Leadership

As an entrepreneur, you are the driving force and visionary leader of your business. Your role extends beyond generating ideas—it encompasses setting a clear direction, fostering a healthy organizational culture, and guiding your team through daily operations and long-term strategy. Effective leadership is more than the ability to inspire—it requires a comprehensive set of management competencies, including communication, organization, time management, strategic planning, resilience, problem-solving, and foundational knowledge in sales, marketing, accounting, and customer services.

Essential Entrepreneurial Skills

Communication

Strong communication skills are essential for sharing information clearly and persuasively across various channels. Whether interacting with vendors, investors, customers, or employees, entrepreneurs must be able to articulate their vision, explain complex ideas, and cultivate trust. Good communication strengthens relationships and facilitates effective collaboration.

Organization

Organizational skills enable entrepreneurs to structure tasks, allocate resources efficiently, and align business operations with strategic objectives. Being well-organized helps streamline processes, reduce waste, and move closer to defined goals.

Time Management

Entrepreneurs often juggle multiple responsibilities. Prioritizing tasks and managing time effectively ensures that critical initiatives receive proper focus. Time management also supports objective, data-driven decision-making and enhances overall productivity.

Strategic Thinking

Strategic thinking allows entrepreneurs to identify opportunities and threats, adapt to market changes, and make informed decisions. It includes the ability to analyze trends, set long-term goals, and develop tactics that position the business for success.

Resilience

Resilience is a core trait of successful entrepreneurs. Navigating setbacks, learning from failures, and recovering quickly from challenges are all part of the entrepreneurial journey. Rather than viewing failure as defeat, resilient entrepreneurs treat it as a preparation for future success.

Problem-solving

Effective problem-solving involves tackling both immediate issues and long-term obstacles, using structured approaches that lead to sustainable results.

Core Functional Knowledge

Even if you delegate operations, understanding key areas such as sales, marketing, accounting, and customer service is vital.

These disciplines are the backbone of your business and must be understood to ensure strategic oversight and informed leadership.

Customer Focus

Exceptional customer service begins with understanding your target audience. Knowing their needs, preferences, and pain points enables you to create meaningful connections and tailor solutions that deliver real value.

Developing Leadership Capability

Leadership skills evolve over time. Many first-time entrepreneurs feel uncertain leading a team; this is normal and represents a valuable opportunity for growth. Reflect on your strengths and weaknesses, seek feedbacks, and establish specific goals to develop your leadership capacity.

Recognizing and Validating Opportunities

Starting a business with a compelling idea does not guarantee success. A viable business opportunity solves a specific consumer problem and generates value exceeding the required investment. To determine whether an idea is commercially sound, conduct thorough market research, identify your target customers, test your product or service, and develop realistic financial projections.

If early feedback is unfavorable, don't abandon your idea—refine it. You may uncover a more promising business model or target market through this process. Once a concept is validated, ongoing evaluation is necessary to adjust to emerging opportunities or threats.

Gaining Insight Through Experience

Entrepreneurs have a unique ability to perceive potential where others do not. However, this vision is often shaped through trial and error. As you operate your business, your insight will sharpen through real-world experience—reviewing financial performance, analyzing market data, and refining your strategic plans. Over time, you will better assess the viability of opportunities and determine the resources needed for success.

Business Development Timelines

Statistically, many new businesses face a one-to-three-year proving period during which viability is determined. Sustainable ventures require time and persistence to grow. Recognize that successful entrepreneurs did not achieve results overnight—they developed their skills, navigated setbacks, and consistently built on experience.

Creating a Business Plan

A strong business plan begins with a clear mission and well-defined objectives. Without this foundational clarity, it is easy to lose direction or become discouraged when challenges arise. Your business plan should:

- Define your value proposition
- Estimate startup and operating costs (salaries, rent, insurance, licensing, and so on)
- Choose a legal business structure (for example, sole proprietorship, partnership, corporation, or as a Limited Liability Company [LLC])
- Outline goals and timelines
- Identify competitive advantages and market positioning
- Explain how the business will make money and grow

Targeting Customers

With a business concept in mind, the next step is identifying your target customers. If entering an established market, analyze existing competitors and look for saturation. Consider how to differentiate your offering. Ask:

- What are competitors doing well that you can emulate?
- What areas can you outperform them in?
- How will you stand out?

If introducing an entirely new product or service, focus on educating and exciting potential customers. Gauge market readiness—if your innovation is too advanced or the economic environment is unfavorable, adoption may be slow.

Market research is critical. Study consumer behavior, assess unmet needs, and determine which features or benefits resonate most. Develop detailed customer personas and conduct surveys or interviews to refine your understanding. The goal is to define and attract your ideal customer segment.

Designing the Business

Once you've validated your idea and target audience, design the business model and develop a prototype or MVP. This step is essential to secure investor interest and demonstrate feasibility.

A formal business plan should articulate short- and long-term goals, how you'll achieve them, and the timeframe for success. Even if some assumptions remain uncertain, a structured plan is indispensable for fundraising and internal guidance.

Building Your Network

Every successful entrepreneur benefits from a strong network of mentors, advisors, partners, and investors. Seek guidance from industry experts, legal counsel, and financial advisors. Early-stage funding may come from personal connections, such as friends and family, so building trust and clearly communicating your business plan is essential.

Securing Funding

Launching a business requires capital—for development, production, operations, and marketing. Funding options vary depending on your industry and growth plans:

- *Self-funding*: Offers full control but carries a personal financial risk.
- *Friends and Family*: May offer favorable terms but rely on personal relationships and trust.
- *Bank Loans*: Require detailed business plans and are often collateral.
- *Small Business Administration (SBA) Loans/Alternative Lenders*: Support small businesses with accessible terms.
- *Grants*: Highly competitive but do not require repayment; often available for underrepresented groups.
- *Angel Investors/Venture Capital*: Ideal for startups with high growth potential. Requires a compelling business case and willingness to share ownership.
- *Crowdfunding*: Uses platforms like Indiegogo, Wefunder, and StartEngine to raise small amounts from many contributors.

Establishing Operations

With funding secured, establish your business infrastructure. This includes:

- Choosing a physical location or remote setup
- Creating a professional website and digital presence
- Structuring your organization
- Incorporating as an LLC or other legal entity to protect personal assets

Avoid over-leveraging your personal credit to finance the business. Registering the business properly limits liability and improves credibility.

Commercialization

What marks the phase where your concept transitions into a tangible business is commercialization. At this point, you should have finalized the product design, completed quality assurance testing, and developed a cohesive marketing strategy. With these steps completed, you are now prepared to bring your product to market.

A crucial step is selecting a business name. Choose a name that is simple, memorable, and legally available for registration. Avoid names that are already trademarked or in use by another entity. Additionally, ensure the name is broad enough to accommodate potential future expansion, rather than limiting the scope of your business.

Post-commercialization Strategy

Marketing and promotion are not one-time tasks but ongoing efforts. The initial buzz from a product launch can generate excitement, but sustained growth requires consistent outreach and communication. Continue refining your marketing approach based on data from campaign metrics and social media analytics. This iterative evaluation helps determine which strategies are effective and which need adjustment.

Early adopters can become brand advocates if you successfully engage them. Their enthusiasm can extend your reach through word-of-mouth referrals and positive online reviews—both valuable tools for long-term brand credibility and customer acquisition.

Establishing an Online Presence

In today's business landscape, having a website is essential, even for businesses that do not operate primarily online. Secure a domain name that reflects your brand identity before it becomes unavailable. Leverage social media platforms that align with your target audience—such as Facebook, Instagram, X (formerly Twitter), and YouTube—and ensure that your activity on these platforms is consistent and strategic.

Avoid spreading yourself too thin. Instead, select platforms you can manage effectively and tailor your content to match the interests and behaviors of your audience. Regular updates, relevant messaging, and thoughtful engagement are essential to maintaining visibility and credibility.

Exploring the Franchise Option

If launching a business from scratch seems overwhelming, consider purchasing a franchise. Franchising offers a proven business model, brand recognition, and operational support. This structured environment can be appealing to those seeking entrepreneurship with reduced uncertainty.

However, franchising also limits autonomy. Franchisees must follow established guidelines and typically have less flexibility to innovate. The decision to invest in a franchise should align with your background, financial resources, and personal business goals.

Franchise businesses often secure financing more easily through loans or grants because of their lower risk profile. A solid business plan further increases the likelihood of securing funding. While banks prefer steady, reliable returns, venture capitalists usually look for high-growth potential and scalability.

Common Pitfalls in Entrepreneurship

Starting a business involves substantial risk, and statistics show that a significant percentage of new ventures fail within the first few years. Only about 15 percent of startups deliver substantial returns to investors. Many either dissolve or manage only modest sustainability without delivering notable profits.

Common reasons for failure include:

- *Poor initial planning*: With too many strategic choices, founders may struggle to identify the best course of action, resulting in abrupt changes and spiraling costs.
- *Excessive debt*: High-interest loans can severely limit a company's ability to scale or generate profit.
- *Inflexibility*: Markets and environments evolve rapidly. Businesses must be prepared to adapt their strategies to stay relevant and competitive.
- *Internal conflict*: Disagreements between founders or with employees can halt progress and even lead to dissolution. Managing workplace culture and maintaining professional, open communication is critical to success.

While some entrepreneurs prefer to operate without a co-founder to retain full control, this path requires strong leadership and clarity in expectations with team members and investors. The advantage lies in full equity ownership and streamlined decision-making. However, solo founders may lack support in times of high pressure.

Conversely, having co-founders can bring diverse skills, share responsibilities, and ease access to funding. A well-aligned partnership can help navigate early-stage challenges and foster innovation through collaborative problem-solving.

Enhancing Entrepreneurial Competence

Entrepreneurs can benefit significantly from formal education and training. For instance, the University of San Diego offers a Master of Science in Innovation, Technology, and Entrepreneurship—a joint program between the School of Business and School of Engineering. Such programs are designed to help aspiring innovators to bring their ideas to life by combining technical acumen with business strategy.

Entrepreneurial Success Stories

There is no single formula for entrepreneurial success. Every success story begins with an idea, but the journey from concept to impact involves dedication, strategic thinking, and resilience. By studying the experiences of successful entrepreneurs, aspiring founders can gain valuable insights into best practices, decision-making frameworks, and potential pitfalls.

Adi Dassler: Adidas

Adi Dassler began making shoes in his mother's washroom in a small Bavarian town with the vision of creating the best athletic footwear. He actively sought feedback from athletes to improve his designs. In 1949, he founded "Adi Dassler Adidas Sportschuhfabrik", and registered the now-iconic three-stripe trademark.

His breakthrough came in 1954, when the German national football team won the World Cup wearing Adidas cleats. The victory catapulted Adidas to global recognition. Dassler's relentless customer focus and willingness to adapt his designs based on user needs set a precedent for product-driven innovation.

"Adi Dassler's secret to success had an additional personal ingredient: he met with athletes, listened carefully, and constantly observed what could be improved or invented to support their needs."— Adidas

Neil Blumenthal: Warby Parker

As a Wharton Master of Business Administration (MBA) student, Neil Blumenthal lost his prescription glasses and was frustrated by the high replacement cost. This inconvenience sparked an idea: to offer affordable, stylish eyewear online. He partnered with classmates Dave Gilboa, Andy Hunt, and Jeff Raider to launch Warby Parker.

Their concept—online ordering, home try-ons, and social responsibility—disrupted a stagnant market. Within weeks of launching, the company hit its first-year sales target and had a waitlist of over 20,000 customers. Warby Parker's success stemmed from market disruption, affordability, user-centric design, and its buy-one-donate-one model.

Jeff Bezos: Amazon

Jeff Bezos left a successful Wall Street career after recognizing the explosive potential of the internet. In 1994, he founded Amazon as an online bookstore from his garage in Seattle. His early vision extended beyond books to a full-scale online retail platform.

Customer satisfaction was Bezos's top priority. His innovations—such as Amazon Prime, one-click ordering, and 24/7 service—created a seamless experience that fueled the company's growth into the world's largest e-commerce business.

Beyond Amazon, Bezos founded *Blue Origin*, acquired *The Washington Post*, and launched initiatives like the *Bezos Earth Fund*, demonstrating his commitment to innovation, media, and environmental causes.

"Amazon is the world's best place to fail. Unless you're not afraid to fail, you can't experiment. And if you don't experiment, you don't invent."— Jeff Bezos

Bill Gates: Microsoft

Bill Gates's journey began in high school, where he and Paul Allen collaborated on software projects. After dropping out of Harvard, they founded Microsoft to develop BASIC software for microcomputers. Microsoft's big break came when it created the Microsoft Disk Operating System, commonly known as the MS-DOS operating system, followed by the revolutionary Windows Graphic User Interface (GUI).

Microsoft's success lay in providing high-quality, adaptable software to manufacturers. Gates's strategy, vision, and partnerships propelled Microsoft into dominance. The company's Initial Public Offering (IPO) brought in $61 million, making Gates one of the richest individuals in the world.

Although Gates did not invent a new product, he identified and filled a critical need in computing. He later noted:

"Success is a lousy teacher. It seduces smart people into thinking they can't lose."

Gates encourages entrepreneurs to learn from both success and failure. Innovation, adaptability, and continuous learning have defined his legacy.

Elon Musk

Widely regarded as one of the most influential entrepreneurs of the modern era, Elon Musk was born in South Africa. He demonstrated entrepreneurial talent at just 12 years of age when he created and sold a video game to a computer magazine. After earning degrees in physics and economics from the University of Pennsylvania, Musk moved to California to pursue business opportunities in the burgeoning tech industry.

In 1995, he co-founded Zip2, a software company that was later sold for $307 million. Following that success, he launched X.com, an online payment company that eventually became PayPal after a merger. In 2002, PayPal was acquired by eBay for $1.5 billion. That same year, Musk founded SpaceX with the goal of making space travel more affordable. In 2004, he joined Tesla Motors as its product architect and became its CEO in 2008. His other ventures include co-founding SolarCity, a solar energy services company; launching Neuralink, a neurotechnology company; founding The Boring Company, which develops underground transportation tunnels; supporting the creation of OpenAI; and more recently, acquiring Twitter and rebranding it as "X".

Musk advocates a clear and disciplined mindset: "*Simplify before you optimize, accelerate only after clarity, and automate as the final touch.*" His approach emphasizes focus and efficiency in solving complex business problems.

Musk exemplifies serial entrepreneurship. From video games and online banking to electric vehicles and space exploration, he has consistently pushed the boundaries of innovation. His success stems from a unique combination of visionary thinking, strategic risk-taking, technical acumen, and a desire to make a global impact. He believes failure is a necessary part of innovation, once stating, "*If you're not failing, you're not innovating enough.*"

Musk's ambitions consistently aim to transform the world—whether through sustainable energy, space colonization, or advanced transportation systems. He expects his teams to mirror his own values: bold vision, relentless innovation, and the courage to challenge the status quo. For entrepreneurs like Musk, financial gain is secondary to the impact and legacy of their work.

Steve Jobs

Steve Jobs, co-founder of Apple Inc., is remembered as one of the most visionary entrepreneurs in history. Raised by adoptive parents in Cupertino, California—now the heart of Silicon Valley—Jobs briefly attended Reed College in Oregon before dropping out. He worked at Atari as a video game designer and later reconnected with high school friend, Steve Wozniak, who was building his own computer.

Using funds raised from selling personal belongings, the pair built the Apple I in Jobs's family garage. In 1977, they launched the Apple II, which became one of the first mass-market personal computers and marked the company's entry into mainstream success. By 1983, Apple had secured a place on the Fortune 500 list.

Despite early success, Jobs faced major setbacks. In 1985, he was ousted from Apple—a turning point that he later described as liberating. He went on to acquire a struggling animation studio, which became Pixar. Under Jobs's leadership, Pixar emerged as a global leader in animated entertainment.

Apple faltered in his absence and neared bankruptcy by the mid-1990s. Jobs returned in 1997 and led a remarkable turnaround, introducing breakthrough products such as the iMac, iPod, iPhone, and iPad. These innovations revolutionized personal computing, music, and telecommunications, solidifying Apple's reputation as a design and innovation powerhouse.

One of Jobs's key strengths was his ability to simplify complex technologies and make them accessible and elegant. He also had the foresight to disrupt Apple's own products before competitors could—most notably with the iPad, which outpaced the need for traditional laptops.

At the time of his passing in 2011, Jobs had transformed Apple into the world's most valuable company. His legacy is defined by his relentless pursuit of excellence, insistence on simplicity, and unwavering belief in the power of innovation. Jobs's journey reminds aspiring entrepreneurs that vision, resilience, and the courage to challenge conventional thinking can lead to profound change.

Richard Branson

Sir Richard Branson's entrepreneurial journey is a story of resilience, bold risk-taking, and extraordinary ambition. Despite facing financial struggles in his youth—including two bankruptcies before the age of 18—Branson persevered, relying on instinct, creativity, and charisma to build an empire.

Branson overcame both dyslexia and a lack of formal education by honing his interpersonal skills and trusting his intuition. At the age of 16, he launched a student magazine, which eventually led to the creation of the Virgin Group—a multinational conglomerate that today spans music, aviation, telecommunications, health, and even space tourism.

Among his ventures, Branson took on the challenge of reviving a struggling airline, which became the successful Virgin Atlantic. Though he faced fierce competition and significant financial pressures, his commitment to service innovation—such as offering superior in-flight experiences—helped differentiate his brand.

Branson is known for embracing unconventional ideas and promoting a culture of innovation. He encourages his teams to think creatively and pursue transformative solutions. One of his most ambitious initiatives is Virgin Galactic, which aims to make space travel accessible to civilians.

Despite numerous setbacks, Branson's unwavering optimism and ability to learn from failure have fueled his continued success. His story is a powerful example for aspiring entrepreneurs: with determination, self-belief, and the courage to take calculated risks, it is possible to overcome obstacles and achieve extraordinary outcomes.

Eric Yuan

As the founder of Zoom Video Communications, Eric Yuan embodies a story of persistence, vision, and global impact. Growing up in a modest household in rural China, Yuan worked in local factories during the day and studied English at night. Inspired by a speech from Bill Gates during his college years, he aspired to join the tech industry in the US.

After being denied a visa multiple times, Yuan was finally granted entry into the US, where he began working at WebEx, a video conferencing company. Rising through the ranks to become the VP of Engineering, Yuan built a global team of over 800 engineers and helped grow company revenues to $700 million.

Frustrated by WebEx's limitations and the upper management's resistance to innovation, Yuan envisioned a new, mobile-friendly video conferencing platform. When his proposal was rejected, he made the bold decision to leave and start his own company. That company became Zoom.

Zoom launched its first product in 2012, gaining one million users within a year. During the COVID-19 pandemic, Zoom became a critical communication tool, growing from 10 million to over 300 million daily meeting participants. Yuan's net worth surged to over $30 billion.

Yuan attributes his success to passion, technical expertise, and a willingness to take personal risks. His story is a testament to the power of perseverance, the importance of customer-focused innovation, and the potential for a single idea to change the way the world connects.

Conclusion

Entrepreneurship is a dynamic journey that blends vision, resilience, and execution. It challenges individuals to solve problems, adapt to change, and create lasting value—often through trial, failure, and growth. With determination, continuous learning, and a clear sense of purpose, any aspiring entrepreneur has the potential to turn an idea into impact and build a legacy of innovation.

9

The Intrapreneur

Driving Innovation from Within

Intrapreneurship is the practice of fostering entrepreneurial thinking and innovation within the framework of an established organization. An *intrapreneur* is an employee who takes the initiative to develop new products, services, or processes that add value to the organization. While they operate within a company's existing structure, intrapreneurs think and act like entrepreneurs—demonstrating creativity, initiative, and a passion for solving problems.

Intrapreneurs are known for their ability to collaborate across departments, navigate internal processes, and gain support for innovative initiatives. They are resourceful, motivated, and proactive, often leading internal projects that drive competitive advantage. Though they work with less personal risk than entrepreneurs, they also operate with fewer freedoms and must align their vision with the company's strategic goals.

> An *intrapreneur* is an employee who takes the initiative to develop new products, services, or processes that add value to the organization.

Origin and Evolution

The term *intrapreneurship* was first introduced in the 1970s in a paper titled "Intra-corporate Entrepreneurship". While entrepreneurs were creating new ventures from scratch, intrapreneurs were transforming corporations from within. Since then, the concept has expanded to include startups, nonprofits, and public sector organizations. Today, intrapreneurship varies significantly across industries, geographies, and organizational cultures, but its core purpose remains the same: fostering innovation internally.

Characteristics of Intrapreneurs

An intrapreneur shares many qualities with an entrepreneur—such as creativity, risk tolerance, and drive—but chooses to apply these traits within an existing organization. They may lead internal innovations, champion new product development, or even establish new business units. Unlike entrepreneurs, intrapreneurs benefit from the organization's infrastructure, resources, and safety net, although they typically have less autonomy. Some intrapreneurs see their role as a stepping stone to eventually launching their own ventures.

Benefits and Challenges

Intrapreneurs face reduced personal risk and maintain job security, yet their financial rewards may be less significant than those of entrepreneurs. Still, they gain recognition, career advancement, and the satisfaction of contributing to the organization's growth. As innovation becomes essential for sustained competitiveness, businesses increasingly recognize the importance of intrapreneurship in driving internal transformation and adaptability.

Despite its benefits, intrapreneurship is often underutilized. Surveys show that fewer than one-third of employees feel empowered to innovate. Organizations must foster a culture that welcomes new ideas, experimentation, and continuous improvement. Failure to do so can have long-term consequences, as illustrated by the case of Kodak. Despite inventing the first digital camera, Kodak rejected the innovation for fear it would disrupt its film business—and as a result, it ultimately lost relevance in the digital age.

Intrapreneurship as a Business Imperative

To remain agile and responsive in today's rapidly evolving business landscape, companies must support employees who think beyond their job descriptions. Intrapreneurship empowers individuals to pursue innovative ideas, take calculated risks, and solve pressing problems within the organization. This internal drive for improvement enhances responsiveness to market changes and positions companies for sustained success.

Support for intrapreneurs includes providing the tools, funding, mentorship, and autonomy necessary to experiment and iterate on new concepts. Innovation labs, dedicated project teams, and cross-functional collaborations are common methods for institutionalizing intrapreneurship within companies.

Cultivating a Culture of Intrapreneurship

A successful intrapreneurial culture requires organizational commitment at every level. This includes leadership buy-in, formal recognition of intrapreneurial contributions, and systems to capture and implement employee-driven ideas. Recognition may take the form of financial incentives, promotions, or public acknowledgement, all of which reinforce the value of innovation.

To ensure success, organizations should also provide structured opportunities for employees to share and test their ideas. This includes innovation workshops, regular brainstorming sessions, and feedback mechanisms that engage all levels of staff. Creating space for ideation and experimentation can turn passive employees into active intrapreneurs.

Skills and Traits of Successful Intrapreneurs

Intrapreneurs possess a unique blend of traits and competencies that allow them to thrive within organizations:

- *Creativity*: They think outside the box and generate novel ideas.
- *Risk-taking*: They are willing to explore untested ideas and take calculated risks.
- *Proactivity*: Intrapreneurs do not wait for permission; they seek opportunities and act on them.
- *Resilience*: They persist through setbacks and adapt to obstacles.
- *Communication*: They can effectively advocate their ideas and influence stakeholders.
- *Project Management*: They plan, budget, and execute initiatives within time and resource constraints.
- *Organizational Acumen*: They understand internal dynamics and build alliances to gain support.
- *Collaboration*: Intrapreneurs work cross-functionally and rely on teamwork to realize their vision.
- *Continuous Learning*: They stay informed and develop new skills to stay ahead of emerging trends.

Empowering Intrapreneurs for Organizational Growth

Promoting intrapreneurship begins by creating an environment that encourages entrepreneurial thinking. This includes training in strategic thinking, risk management, and problem-solving, as well as establishing clear pathways for employees to propose and lead innovation initiatives. Recognizing and rewarding contributions reinforces the behavior and builds momentum.

Organizations can institutionalize intrapreneurship by establishing innovation hubs, providing seed funding for employee-led projects, and appointing mentors to guide intrapreneurs through execution. These resources help translate creative ideas into actionable solutions, creating long-term value.

However, a lack of support, resources, or recognition can hinder intrapreneurial efforts. To avoid this, companies must invest in their innovators and ensure they have the time, autonomy, and backing needed to succeed.

Intrapreneurship: Unlocking Innovation from Within

Fostering Creativity and Innovation

At the heart of every successful business lies innovation—the ability to discover faster, better, and more cost-effective methods to deliver products and services. Intrapreneurship is the practice of leveraging the mindset of entrepreneurial employees within an organization, empowering them to generate and pursue innovative ideas. It nurtures a culture where creativity thrives, experimentation is encouraged, and employees feel ownership over their contributions.

Intrapreneurs are natural problem-solvers and opportunity-seekers. They identify inefficiencies, improve existing offerings, develop novel solutions, and challenge the status quo. This mindset drives continuous improvement and ensures that companies remain dynamic and competitive. By enabling employees to lead initiatives from concept to execution, organizations benefit from increased innovation, enhanced problem-solving, and the development of high-value products, services, and internal processes.

Driving Competitive Advantage

Intrapreneurs often operate on the frontier of a company's core activities, identifying blind spots, emerging trends, and untapped markets. Their proactive approach allows them to spot opportunities and threats that may otherwise be overlooked. In this way, intrapreneurship becomes a strategic advantage, positioning companies to respond to shifts in the market with agility and foresight.

Moreover, when employees are entrusted with responsibility and autonomy, they develop a greater sense of ownership. This often leads to higher motivation, stronger engagement, and a commitment to achieving excellence. Empowered employees are more likely to take initiative, contribute innovative ideas, and execute them effectively—ultimately increasing efficiency and organizational effectiveness.

Fueling Organizational Growth

In a rapidly evolving business landscape, the ability to adapt and grow is essential. Intrapreneurship helps businesses remain competitive by tapping into the innovative capacity of their workforce. By encouraging employees to take calculated risks and propose disruptive ideas, organizations gain access to a powerful engine of growth.

In contrast to traditional models where ideation is confined to R&D departments, intrapreneurial companies welcome ideas from all levels. This inclusive approach fosters a constant stream of innovation, enabling companies to launch new products, enter new markets, and refine operational strategies to drive sustained growth.

Enhancing Talent Acquisition and Retention

Intrapreneurship plays a critical role in attracting and retaining top talent. Forward-thinking professionals—especially younger generations—seek roles that offer purpose, autonomy, and opportunities for innovation. A workplace that values employee creativity and provides platforms for meaningful contribution is more likely to retain engaged and inspired individuals.

Research from Gallup shows that engaged employees are more productive and significantly less likely to leave their roles. Intrapreneurship provides this engagement by granting employees the ability to influence change, solve real problems, and align their personal passions with organizational goals. This fosters loyalty, increases morale, and strengthens the overall employee experience.

Intrapreneurship also serves as a leadership pipeline, allowing companies to identify high-potential individuals. By profiling and celebrating intrapreneurial success stories, organizations enhance their employer brand and become magnets for like-minded, innovation-driven talent.

Boosting Profitability and Efficiency

When employees think and act like entrepreneurs, they are naturally aligned with the organization's bottom line. Intrapreneurs evaluate ideas based on impact and feasibility—prioritizing profitability, efficiency, and scalability. They are resourceful, often finding cost-effective solutions and identifying process improvements that reduce waste and increase productivity.

This focus on value creation leads to the development of MVPs, rapid prototyping, and iterative refinement based on customer feedback. By shortening the product development cycle, intrapreneurs reduce time-to-market and improve responsiveness to consumer needs—resulting in cost savings and increased revenue streams.

Promoting Agility and Adaptability

Agility is a competitive necessity in today's business environment. Intrapreneurs bring adaptability by continuously scanning the external environment, anticipating future trends, and reacting swiftly to change. Their ability to think creatively and mobilize teams quickly enables organizations to pivot strategies and seize emerging opportunities.

Because intrapreneurs are embedded within the company, they possess intimate knowledge of internal processes, making implementation faster and more effective. Their ability to work across departments, overcome resistance, and leverage existing resources makes them invaluable change agents.

Strengthening Organizational Culture

Intrapreneurship contributes to a dynamic and resilient organizational culture. Employees who are encouraged to innovate and lead, gain a deeper sense of purpose in their roles. Their enthusiasm becomes contagious, fostering team collaboration, cross-functional learning, and a shared commitment to success.

As successful intrapreneurial ventures accumulate, they serve as internal case studies—reinforcing a culture of innovation, accountability, and continuous improvement. Organizations that champion such initiatives become more attractive to external stakeholders, including investors, partners, and prospective employees.

Empowering Employee Development

For individual employees, intrapreneurship is a powerful tool for personal and professional growth. It offers opportunities to acquire critical skills such as project management, leadership, creativity, and resilience. Intrapreneurs often experience higher job satisfaction, a greater sense of fulfillment, and increased visibility within the organization.

Moreover, they are more likely to be recognized and rewarded for their contributions. Successful projects can lead to career advancement, internal promotions, or new leadership responsibilities—all these further reinforcing their commitment to the organization.

Managing Innovation with Strategy and Patience

While intrapreneurship thrives on bold ideas and experimentation, it also requires discipline and strategic alignment. Not every idea will succeed immediately—and failure is part of the innovation process. Intrapreneurs must develop resilience, learn from setbacks, and remain patient while refining their solutions.

Clear communication with the leadership about expectations and success criteria is essential. Establishing a shared understanding of risk tolerance, project goals, and metrics for evaluation ensures that intrapreneurs are supported and trusted, even when outcomes are uncertain.

Intrapreneurship: A Growing Force of Innovation Within Organizations

The Rise of Intrapreneurship

Intrapreneurship—the act of behaving like an entrepreneur within a large organization—is becoming an increasingly prevalent trend across industries. Forward-thinking companies are creating internal innovation platforms and programs that empower employees to launch entrepreneurial ventures from within, aiming to accelerate innovation and respond more dynamically to market demands.

This shift is not merely a strategic evolution but also a response to talent retention challenges. Large corporations have seen many of their most talented employees leave to pursue independent startup ventures, driven by a desire for autonomy, creative expression, and meaningful problem-solving. To counter this, companies are embracing intrapreneurship as a way to provide employees with similar opportunities for ownership and innovation, without requiring them to leave the organization.

Creating a Culture of Intrapreneurship

Organizations that succeed in fostering intrapreneurship typically build a culture that values creativity, risk-taking, and employee empowerment. These companies offer time, resources, and organizational support for intrapreneurs to explore new ideas. Employees are encouraged to think beyond their job descriptions and take ownership of innovative solutions. The result is a more agile and resilient enterprise, capable of maintaining competitive advantage in a constantly evolving marketplace.

By embedding intrapreneurial values into their culture, companies stimulate organic innovation and create pathways for product development, operational efficiency, and new business models. This not only leads to the introduction of groundbreaking solutions but also fosters higher employee engagement and retention.

Notable Intrapreneurship Success Stories

Frito-Lay: Richard Montañez and Flamin' Hot Cheetos

Richard Montañez, who started working in Frito-Lay as a janitor, took to heart the CEO's call for employees to "act like an owner". Observing a lack of products tailored to Latino consumers, he developed the concept for Flamin' Hot Cheetos. Without a formal education or product development role, he pitched his idea directly to the leadership in companies. The snack became one of Frito-Lay's most successful products, and Montañez rose to become the VP of Cultural Sales. His journey exemplifies how intrapreneurship can empower individuals at every level to make transformative contributions.

Google: Paul Buchheit and Gmail

Google's "20 Percent Time" policy allows employees to dedicate a portion of their workweek to personal innovation projects. Paul Buchheit used this time to develop Gmail, an email platform that integrated powerful search functionality—a concept initially met with internal skepticism. Gmail went on to revolutionize email communication and advertising, playing a pivotal role in the development of Google AdSense and generating substantial revenue. Gmail remains one of Google's most successful intrapreneurial ventures, with over 1.5 billion users worldwide.

Vimeo: Anjali Sud's Strategic Pivot

When Anjali Sud joined Vimeo, the company was struggling and considering launching a streaming service to compete with Netflix. Sud envisioned a different path: a platform for businesses to create and manage video content. She received approval to test her idea with a small team, and her vision ultimately transformed Vimeo's business model. Within a year, sales increased by 54 percent, and subscriber growth rose by 25 percent. Sud's intrapreneurial leadership led her to become Vimeo's CEO and repositioned the company for sustained success.

Sony: Ken Kutaragi and the PlayStation

Ken Kutaragi, a Sony engineer, saw untapped potential in the gaming industry after observing his daughter play on a Nintendo console. Despite initial resistance from the Sony leadership, Kutaragi continued developing a gaming concept, even collaborating secretly with Nintendo. Eventually, Sony supported his efforts, resulting in the development of the PlayStation. The console revolutionized home gaming, and by 2018, Sony had sold over 525 million units. Kutaragi's persistence led to the creation of Sony Interactive Entertainment, where he became the Chairman and CEO.

Airbus: Mina Bastawros and Crowdcraft

Airbus intrapreneur Mina Bastawros launched *Crowdcraft*, a crowdsourcing and crowd-staffing platform designed to solve complex technical challenges through external collaboration. The initiative tapped into global innovation networks and helped Airbus cut project development time by 59 percent and costs by 61 percent. Crowdcraft represents a successful example of ecosystem innovation, where intrapreneurship extends beyond company boundaries to embrace open innovation. Bastawros was promoted to the position of the VP of Creative and Digital Marketing for his contributions.

BASF: BOXLAB Services Spin-off

BOXLAB Services originated from BASF's internal innovation incubator, *Chemovator*, which enables employees to test new business ideas in a safe environment. Intrapreneurs Mischa Feig and Lisa Ruffin developed a solution for replacing damaged packaging and labels in the chemical industry, reducing supply chain complexity, cost, and waste. The project evolved into BOXLAB Services, BASF's first corporate spin-off, now serving over 70 warehouses in 10 countries. This case exemplifies how intrapreneurship can lead to independent, revenue-generating ventures.

3M: The Birth of the Post-it Note

Spencer Silver, a 3M scientist, accidentally discovered a weak adhesive while attempting to create a strong one. Initially considered a "solution without a problem", the invention found its purpose when colleague Art Fry used it to create temporary bookmarks. Fry leveraged 3M's policy allowing time for creative exploration and helped turn the concept into the now-iconic Post-it Note. The product became a commercial success, and Fry is celebrated as a model intrapreneur who identified and executed a transformative idea from within.

Amazon: Charlie Ward and Prime

Amazon Prime, one of the company's most influential services, originated from an idea proposed by principal engineer Charlie Ward. Frustrated by a clunky checkout process, Ward suggested a streamlined shipping model. Jeff Bezos championed the idea and assembled a secret team to develop what was initially called "Futurama". Despite internal skepticism, Amazon Prime launched and transformed the e-commerce landscape, setting new standards for customer loyalty and shipping expectations.

McDonald's: Bob Bernstein and the Happy Meal

In the late 1970s, McDonald's marketing executive Bob Bernstein sought to attract more families to the fast-food chain. Recognizing a gap in offerings for children, he created the *Happy Meal*, bundling child-sized food portions with a toy. Introduced in 1979, the Happy Meal became a cultural staple and one of McDonald's most successful innovations, with approximately one billion sold each year.

Conclusion

Intrapreneurship is not merely a trend or buzzword—it is a strategic imperative for organizations seeking long-term innovation, growth, and resilience.

Intrapreneurs are the often-unsung heroes who drive transformation from within, using their deep understanding of company systems, processes, and customer needs to identify new opportunities and develop breakthrough solutions. From janitors to engineers to marketers, intrapreneurs come from all levels of an organization and prove that innovation thrives when curiosity, initiative, and support converge.

Organizations that foster a culture of intrapreneurship—by providing resources, autonomy, and encouragement—gain more than just innovative products or services. They experience increased employee engagement, faster time-to-market, and a sharpened competitive edge. Empowering employees to think and act like entrepreneurs unlocks hidden potential and fuels adaptability in a rapidly changing business environment.

Ultimately, cultivating intrapreneurship is about enabling transformation from within. It is a powerful strategy for building a dynamic, future-ready enterprise—one where innovation is not confined to the executive suite, but is embedded in the culture and driven by employees at every level.

10

Disruptive Innovation

Redefining the Competitive Landscape

In today's dynamic business environment, staying ahead of the competition requires more than incremental improvements—it demands breakthrough thinking. While many organizations rely on *sustaining innovation* to improve existing products and services for current customers, *disruptive innovation* takes a fundamentally different approach. It challenges established norms, reshapes markets, and paves the way for new players to outpace industry giants.

Understanding Disruptive Innovation

First introduced by *Harvard Business School professor Clayton Christensen in 1977,* the concept of disruptive innovation explains how new entrants with fewer resources can successfully challenge well-established businesses. Christensen defined disruptive innovation as *"The process by which a product or service takes root initially in simple applications at the bottom of a market and then relentlessly moves upmarket, eventually displacing established competitors."*

These innovations often begin as low-cost or more accessible alternatives that appeal to niche or underserved markets. Over time, they improve in quality and performance, moving upmarket and eventually transforming entire industries.

According to *Indeed.com*, "*...disruptive innovation is the idea that the invention of a new product can disrupt an entire market, changing what customers want out of a business or what employees expect from their employer and vice versa.*"

Examples abound: digital streaming disrupted the traditional video rental and television markets; digital downloads and music platforms displaced physical media; and smartphones redefined personal computing and communication. Disruption is not only about product design—it's about *redefining consumer behavior and business models*.

Disruption as a New Business Trend

Disruptive innovation is not limited to startups. Large enterprises are increasingly aware of its impact. A study by *Accenture*, the global professional services company, found that *60 percent of companies are already experiencing disruption*, while *44 percent are highly susceptible to future disruption*. Meanwhile, *Harvard Business School* emphasizes how smaller companies can challenge dominant incumbents by focusing on agility, innovation, and customer centricity.

Many established businesses focus on their most profitable and demanding customers. This often leaves gaps in the market that startups and newcomers quickly fill—eventually growing to challenge incumbents directly. This "fringe-to-mainstream" evolution is a hallmark of disruptive innovation.

A study by *Forbes*, the US business magazine, reveals that *83 percent of executives*, who identify their organizations as disruptors, report increased revenue, highlighting the competitive advantage of embracing disruption rather than resisting it.

Cautionary Tale: Kodak's Missed Opportunity

One of the most cited examples of failure to adapt is *Kodak*. Despite inventing the digital camera, Kodak resisted its potential for fear of cannibalizing its profitable film business. The company delayed innovation, misjudged the pace of change, and failed to execute a digital transformation strategy. As a result, Kodak lost its leadership position and filed for bankruptcy in 2012.

Kodak's story illustrates how prioritizing short-term gains and resisting change can lead to long-term decline. In contrast, companies like *Netflix*, *Apple*, and *Google* have continuously evolved—disrupting their own business models before competitors could.

The Role of Disruptive Leadership

Disruption is not driven by innovation alone—it also requires *visionary leadership*. As *GovConWire*, which provides informative, breaking business news to government contractual sectors, notes:

> *"Disruptive leadership means that you are always looking for better solutions to your problems and searching for ways to innovate your organization's products, services, and processes."*

> Disruption is not driven by innovation alone—it also requires visionary leadership.

Disruptive leaders challenge the status quo, think beyond traditional boundaries, and foster cultures of experimentation and calculated risk-taking.

Richard Branson, founder of the Virgin Group, exemplifies disruptive leadership. Once dismissed as a disruptive student, Branson used his non-conventional thinking to challenge traditional industries—from airlines to the telecom industry. He famously recalled a school principal telling him, *"You'll either end up in prison or become a millionaire."* Branson's career proves how disruptive thinking, when paired with vision and persistence, can lead to extraordinary success.

However, disruptive leadership comes with challenges. Resistance from employees, customers, or stakeholders is common, especially when major changes are involved. Effective communication, emotional intelligence, and a clear strategic vision are crucial to managing change and aligning teams.

Putting Disruptive Innovation into Practice

Implementing disruptive innovation requires a strategic mindset and supportive organizational structure. Successful disruptive business models typically embrace:

- *Customer-centric Designs*: Understanding unmet needs and creating solutions tailored to overlooked segments.
- *Agility and Adaptability*: Remaining flexible to pivot strategies in response to market changes.
- *Technology and Partnerships*: Leveraging emerging technologies and building value-driven partnerships.
- *Internal Innovation Ecosystems*: Encouraging employees to think like intrapreneurs and take ownership of new ideas.

Startups and new entrants must be nimble, bold, and willing to take risks. For incumbents, the challenge lies in overcoming inertia, embracing change, and investing in internal innovation.

Organizations that recognize emerging trends early, identify potential disruptors, and integrate R&D into their core strategy will be better positioned to thrive in the evolving landscape.

The Risk of Ignoring Disruption

Disruptive innovation doesn't just create opportunities—it also poses existential threats. Companies that ignore these signals risk falling behind or becoming obsolete. The difference between success and failure often comes down to *a willingness to adapt.*

Netflix's transformation from DVD rental service to global streaming powerhouse demonstrates how embracing disruption can lead to market leadership. On the other hand, companies that resist or delay change, like Kodak or Blockbuster, serve as cautionary tales.

Preparing for Disruption

Before embarking on a disruptive innovation journey, companies must take deliberate steps to maximize their chances of success. With only about 5 percent of new consumer products succeeding in the marketplace, organizations must go beyond surface-level market demographics such as age, gender, or income. Instead, they should focus on identifying unmet needs and solving real problems.

Disruptive innovation often requires a departure from conventional corporate structures. Traditional resources, processes, and mindsets may not be suitable for fostering breakthrough ideas. According to innovation leaders, one effective strategy is to establish a dedicated, standalone innovation unit—separate from the core business—that can experiment with new concepts free from institutional constraints. However, this unit should maintain cross-functional communication with the parent organization to ensure that promising innovations can be scaled or integrated when appropriate.

To avoid destructive disruption—where innovation erodes rather than creates value—businesses must pursue disruption constructively. This includes designing innovations that benefit customers, communities, and stakeholders alike. Agile organizational models, such as flattened hierarchies and autonomous cross-functional teams, can accelerate project cycles and minimize bureaucratic delays.

Fostering a Culture of Innovation

Organizational restructuring alone does not drive disruption. A transformative culture is essential—one that embraces experimentation, encourages calculated risk-taking, and treats failure as a learning opportunity rather than a setback.

Companies must be willing to invest in projects that may not yield immediate returns. Encouraging transparency, collaboration, and open feedback cultivates an environment where innovation can flourish. Employees should feel empowered to contribute ideas, challenge assumptions, and engage in rapid iteration.

Supporting this mindset, a study by *Forbes* revealed that 83 percent of executives who view their organizations as disruptors reported notable revenue growth—highlighting the strong correlation between innovation, strategy, and culture.

Challenges and Responsibilities

Disruptive innovation presents significant opportunities—but also considerable risks. Poorly executed disruption can lead to value destruction, alienated stakeholders, and organizational instability. To innovate responsibly, leaders must build agile, execution-focused teams, minimize bureaucratic inertia, and foster a culture of continuous improvement.

Moreover, disruption often generates resistance—from employees, customers, or strategic partners. Leaders must actively listen, communicate transparently, and engage stakeholders throughout the innovation process to build trust and secure alignment.

Types of Disruptive Innovation

Disruptive innovation generally falls into two primary *categories: low-end disruption* and *new-market disruption.*

Low-end Disruption

This type occurs when a company introduces a simpler, more affordable product that appeals to cost-sensitive customers who are over-served by existing solutions. These offerings initially target market segments with limited performance needs but evolve over time to challenge incumbent products. This disruption, while not creating new markets, reallocates market share from high-end products to low-cost alternatives. For example, the personal computer disrupted mainframes by offering affordable, albeit initially less powerful, computing to individual consumers and small businesses. As performance improved, PCs rendered mainframes obsolete for many applications.

New-market Disruption

New-market disruption creates entirely new markets by targeting customers who previously lacked access to a viable solution. These innovations prioritize accessibility, affordability, and convenience over raw performance. They often emerge in overlooked segments and evolve to serve broader markets over time. A prominent example is the iPhone, which redefined mobile computing by combining telephony, internet access, and multimedia functionality into a single device. It created a new smartphone category that fundamentally altered consumer behavior and market expectations.

In both cases, disruptors typically begin with modest capabilities and underserved markets but evolve to dominate through incremental improvements and market realignment. Whether you're leading a mature organization or launching a startup, understanding these patterns is essential for capitalizing on innovation opportunities—or mitigating potential threats.

Identifying Underserved Markets

In today's fast-paced and competitive business environment, the most successful entrepreneurs and companies are those that can spot underserved markets. An underserved market is a segment of consumers or businesses whose needs are not fully met by existing solutions. These markets often represent significant opportunities for innovation and growth.

1. Look for Customer Pain Points

One of the most effective ways to identify underserved markets is by listening closely to customer frustrations with existing products or services. These pain points can be identified through:

- Online reviews and forums
- Social media complaints
- Support ticket analysis
- Customer interviews and surveys

If people are frequently saying things like "*I wish there was a better way to…*" or "*This doesn't work for someone like me*," that's a strong signal of unmet needs.

2. Study Non-consumers

Another rich area for discovering underserved markets is studying non-consumers—people who are not using any existing solutions. This might be due to high cost, complexity, lack of access, or irrelevance. For example, early mobile banking services targeted people without access to traditional banks in emerging markets.

3. Identify Overlooked Niches

Large companies often focus on broad, high-margin customer segments, leaving smaller niches unserved. These overlooked niches might not be profitable for large corporations, but can represent lucrative opportunities for startups or agile businesses.

4. Use Data and Trend Analysis

Market research reports, Google Trends, and analytics tools can provide insights into emerging demands that current players have not yet addressed. Look for fast-growing interest in certain topics or increasing search volume without corresponding product offerings.

5. Map the Value Chain

Sometimes, a market is underserved not in the end product but in a part of the value chain—such as supply, logistics, or financing. By analyzing each link in the chain, businesses can find bottlenecks and inefficiencies to address.

Examples of Underserved Markets

Airbnb: The Unmet Needs in Urban Travel

The Problem

In 2007, major cities around the world were flooded with business travelers and tourists, but hotel capacity was often limited and expensive. At the same time, thousands of city residents had spare bedrooms or empty apartments.

Underserved Market

- Budget-conscious travelers who couldn't afford or didn't want traditional hotels.
- Homeowners or renters with underutilized space who wanted extra income.

How Airbnb Identified the Market

- Founders Brian Chesky and Joe Gebbia saw a personal pain point: they couldn't afford rent in San Francisco, and nearby hotels were fully booked due to a design conference.
- They realized there were no easy platforms for travelers to find short-term, affordable, local lodging—and no way for hosts to monetize extra space.
- Online forums and blogs also revealed growing discontent with high hotel prices and impersonal experiences.

Market Insight

By targeting both travelers and hosts, Airbnb tapped into a large, underserved intersection of demand and supply. Hotels overlooked the budget and community-based segment, creating a gap ripe for disruption.

Paystack: Financial Inclusion in Africa

The Problem

In Nigeria and across Africa, digital payments were notoriously difficult for businesses. Complex bank integrations, the lack of Application Programming Interfaces (APIs), and limited technical support made it hard for startups and Small and Medium Enterprises (SMEs) to collect online payments.

Underserved Market

- Small and medium businesses in Africa.
- Developers and entrepreneurs needing fast and reliable payment infrastructure.

How Paystack Identified the Market

- Founders Shola Akinlade and Ezra Olubi directly experienced the problem as developers.
- They noticed that while businesses in the West had Stripe and PayPal, African businesses lacked developer-friendly payment solutions.
- They observed an increase in online commerce activity across Africa, with little infrastructure to support it.

Market Insight

The opportunity lay not just in payments, but in building trust and the infrastructure for an emerging digital economy.

Google Pay in India as a Disruptive Innovation

The Problem

- Digital transactions in India were once complex and inconvenient.
- Reliance on debit/credit cards, internet banking, and mobile wallets created barriers.
- Extra steps such as recharging wallets or remembering card details discouraged adoption.
- Small merchants and rural users found these methods impractical, continuing to depend on cash.

The Underserved Market

- Millions of Indians had newly opened bank accounts due to financial inclusion initiatives.
- Rapid smartphone penetration meant people had access to digital platforms.
- Despite this, everyday transactions (small purchases, street vendors, local shops) remained largely cash-based.
- Rural communities and small businesses were overlooked by traditional digital payment solutions.

Google Pay's Market Identification

- Recognized that a huge segment of Indians had bank accounts + smartphones, but no simple bridge between the two.
- Saw an opportunity in the government-backed Unified Payments Interface (UPI), which enabled direct, instant, and free bank-to-bank transfers.
- Identified that the pain point was not lack of technology, but the complicated and fragmented experience of existing digital payment systems.

Market Insight

- *Convenience and trust* would determine adoption more than advanced features.
- Users preferred a platform that felt as easy as sending a message.
- First-time digital users needed *confidence-building tools*, such as:
    - Simple, intuitive interface.
    - Local language support.

- o Rewards and cashback to motivate trial and habit formation.

Outcome and Disruption

- Google Pay transformed digital payments into a mainstream activity, accessible to all.
- Brought small merchants, street vendors, and rural users into the digital economy.
- Helped accelerate India's shift toward a cashless economy.
- Set a new benchmark for ease, inclusivity, and scale in financial technology.

Testing Disruptive Innovation Ideas Quickly

Once a potential underserved market is identified, the next step is to test a disruptive innovation idea. Speed is crucial, as it allows innovators to validate assumptions, learn from failures, and iterate with minimal cost.

1. Build a Minimum Viable Product (MVP)

The MVP is a stripped-down version of the product that delivers just enough value to attract early adopters and validate key assumptions. The goal is to learn what works, what doesn't, and whether the market is genuinely interested. An MVP could be a landing page, prototype, or even a concierge-style service.

2. Use the Lean Startup Methodology

The Lean Startup framework encourages building fast, measuring real-world usage, and learning continuously. This approach relies on the *Build-Measure-Learn* loop:

- *Build*: Create a basic version of the product or service.
- *Measure*: Collect data on how users interact with it.
- *Learn*: Analyze the results to refine the product or pivot, if needed.

3. Target Early Adopters

Early adopters are more willing to try new solutions and provide feedback. Engaging with them helps improve the product and build initial traction. These users often become evangelists if the solution effectively addresses their needs.

4. Run Experiments and A/B Tests

To test features or positioning quickly, use controlled experiments or A/B testing. This allows you to determine what changes have a positive impact on user behavior without committing to full development.

5. Pre-sell or Crowdfund

Pre-selling a product before it's fully built or using platforms like Kickstarter can be an effective way to test market demand with minimal upfront investment. It also validates whether people are willing to pay for the solution.

6. Measure Product-market Fit Indicators

Pay attention to early signs of product-market fit, such as:

- High engagement and retention
- Organic growth or word-of-mouth referrals
- Positive feedback and repeated usage

These indicators suggest that the solution resonates with the target market and has potential to scale.

Identifying underserved markets and testing disruptive innovation ideas quickly is both an art and a science. It requires deep empathy for customers, strategic use of data, and a willingness to experiment rapidly. Entrepreneurs and businesses that master these skills can uncover hidden opportunities and develop solutions that challenge the status quo—often leading to significant impact and success. By focusing on real problems and learning fast, innovation becomes not just a buzzword but a sustainable path to growth.

Examples of Testing Disruptive Innovation Ideas Quickly

Case 1: Airbnb: From Air Mattresses to MVP

MVP Approach

- Brian Chesky and Joe Gebbia, both founders of Airbnb, the hospitality company, launched *AirBedAndBreakfast.com* using a simple website offering air mattresses in their apartment.
- The MVP was extremely basic: photos, a description, and a way to pay.
- Their first "guests" were attendees of a design conference who couldn't find hotels.

Rapid Testing

- They collected feedback in person, iterated on their website and service, and verified whether people were willing to pay strangers for short-term lodging.
- To gain trust, they took high-quality photos themselves, acting as a concierge service.

Result

The early MVP validated that people:

- Were willing to stay in strangers' homes.
- Wanted cheaper and more authentic travel experiences.
- Trusted peer reviews more than traditional hotel ratings.

Case 2: Paystack: Build Fast, Prove Value

MVP Approach

- The initial MVP was a basic API that allowed developers to accept payments online in minutes—not weeks.
- It only supported a limited number of payment options (cards and bank transfers) but worked reliably.

Rapid Testing

- The founders demonstrated the MVP live at Y Combinator's Demo Day and accepted beta users right away.
- They actively collected feedback from developers and business owners, rapidly refining their API and dashboard based on real use cases.

Result

- Within a year, Paystack was processing millions in monthly transactions and had secured partnerships with major banks and tech companies.
- It was later acquired by Stripe for over $200 million, underscoring the value of quickly solving real, overlooked problems.

Case 3: Google Pay in India: Simplifying Digital Payments for the Masses

MVP (Minimum Viable Product) Approach

- Google Pay did not attempt to build an entire financial ecosystem at launch.
- Instead, it focused on one *core feature*: instant, free, and secure *bank-to-bank transfers via UPI*. The app minimized friction by avoiding wallets, card details, or complex processes.
- Its MVP was essentially a *simple, clean interface* to make sending money as easy as sending a text.

Rapid Testing

- Launched first in pilot cities to measure adoption and transaction success rates.
- Used incentives (cashback, rewards, referral bonuses) to test whether users would shift from cash to digital transactions.
- Monitored how small merchants, students, and families interacted with the app in *real-life, small-value transactions*.
- Quickly iterated on features like QR code payments, local language support, and security prompts based on feedback.

Result

- Within months, Google Pay gained massive traction, particularly among *underserved segments such as street vendors and rural users*.
- It validated the fact that *simplicity + trust + incentives* could overcome barriers to digital payment adoption.
- Scaled rapidly to become one of India's leading digital payment platforms, transforming the way transactions are

conducted and accelerating the country's move toward a cashless economy.

The Future of Disruptive Innovation

In an increasingly dynamic business landscape, disruptive innovation remains a key strategy for long-term competitiveness. By introducing novel products or services that eventually redefine industry norms, companies can reshape markets and elevate customer expectations.

To stay ahead, organizations must continually invest in R&D, embrace emerging technologies—such as AI, blockchain, 3D printing, and cryptocurrency—and foster adaptable business models. A commitment to monitoring trends, experimenting boldly, and pivoting swiftly is central to remaining competitive.

Disruptive innovation also plays a crucial role in sustainability. Innovative approaches to product design and process efficiency can address pressing environmental concerns while unlocking new business value. For instance, Tesla has reimagined transportation and energy sectors with electric vehicles, solar power, and energy storage—demonstrating how innovation and sustainability can align.

However, disruption carries ethical implications. Job displacement, data privacy, and unintended social consequences must be carefully considered. Companies have a responsibility to innovate ethically, safeguarding stakeholder interests while pursuing growth. The evolution of social media platforms, for example, highlights the importance of transparency and user data protection.

Historical precedents illustrate both cautionary tales and success stories. Kodak's reluctance to embrace digital photography—despite inventing the core technology—serves as a warning against innovation resistance. In contrast, firms like Apple, Google, and

Netflix have demonstrated how strategic reinvention can drive sustained relevance and leadership.

Ultimately, the future of disruption is as promising as it is unpredictable. Organizations that combine visionary leadership, ethical responsibility, and a culture of learning will be best positioned to lead in tomorrow's markets.

Real-world Examples of Disruptive Innovation

Personal Computers

Mainframe computers were initially accessible only to large corporations and universities due to their enormous size and cost. The introduction of personal computers created a new consumer segment by making computing accessible and affordable to individuals. Despite limited capabilities, early PCs met a basic need and rapidly evolved to challenge and eventually replace mainframes.

Smartphones

Smartphones extended computing capabilities into the palm of the hand, disrupting personal computers, landline telephones, cameras, MP3 players, and more. Beyond convenience, smartphones democratized access to the internet and transformed communication, media consumption, and productivity.

Amazon

Amazon revolutionized retail by leveraging e-commerce, logistics, and customer-centric designs. Through innovations such as personalized recommendations, fast delivery, and Prime membership, Amazon forced traditional retailers to reimagine their models, setting a new standard for consumer convenience and efficiency.

Transistor Radios

In the 1950s, Texas Instruments introduced the first transistor radio—small, portable, and affordable—targeting markets ignored by bulky home stereo systems. Although initially of lower audio quality, these radios introduced mobility, eventually leading to further innovations such as the Sony Walkman, MP3 players, and the iPod, which collectively disrupted the in-home audio market.

Shared Mobility Services

An illustrative example of *new-market disruption* has emerged within the automotive industry through the rise of *shared mobility services*. Companies like *Uber, Lyft, Zipcar, Bluebikes,* and *Lime* have created an entirely new market segment by offering transportation alternatives to individuals who either cannot afford or choose not to own a car. These services appeal particularly to urban dwellers for whom car ownership is impractical due to cost, parking limitations, or lifestyle preferences.

While traditional car ownership offers convenience and personal control, shared mobility services provide *flexibility at a significantly lower cost*. Although the performance may not meet the standards of traditional car owners, the value proposition is compelling to this underserved market. For instance, a car owner may find it inconvenient to hail a Lyft or locate a Zipcar; however, for someone without a vehicle, these services offer vastly improved mobility and access.

Uber, in particular, has transformed urban transportation by disrupting traditional taxi services. Its *mobile-first ride-hailing platform*, intuitive user interface, transparent pricing, and real-time driver tracking reshaped customer expectations. Initially adopted by *tech-savvy, younger urban users,* Uber quickly expanded to mainstream consumers, forcing the traditional taxi industry to evolve.

Uber's operational model, driven by scalable technology and *data analytics*, allows for dynamic pricing, optimized route planning, and faster dispatch. Its customer-centric focus and adaptability have made it a textbook example of *disruptive innovation*, effectively challenging and redefining an entrenched industry model.

Netflix

Pioneering the transition from physical DVD rentals to *on-demand streaming services*, Netflix disrupted the entertainment industry by fundamentally transforming how audiences consume television and films. By eliminating the need for physical media and offering a vast, readily accessible content library, Netflix delivered unmatched convenience and personalization.

Beyond streaming, Netflix further disrupted the market by investing in *original content*, such as *Stranger Things* and *The Crown*, attracting loyal subscriber bases and differentiating itself from traditional broadcasters. The company's data-driven approach enables *personalized recommendations*, enhancing user experience and engagement.

Netflix not only anticipated changing consumer behavior but also *accelerated industry-wide transformation*, contributing to the decline of rental giants like Blockbuster and forcing traditional media companies to develop their own streaming platforms.

Airbnb

Founded in 2008, Airbnb revolutionized the hospitality industry by enabling individuals to rent out their homes or rooms through an online marketplace. Initially appealing to *budget-conscious travelers* willing to trade luxury for affordability, Airbnb provided a new market alternative to traditional hotels.

As the platform matured, Airbnb expanded to cater to *higher-end consumers*, offering curated experiences, upscale properties, and business travel accommodations. The company's *asset-light model*, which does not require ownership of rental properties, enabled rapid scalability and cost-efficiency.

Airbnb's value proposition centers on *cost savings, home-like amenities,* and *authentic local experiences,* particularly attractive to leisure travelers seeking immersion over standardization. By leveraging digital technology and a peer-to-peer network, Airbnb has become a prime example of *market-creating disruptive innovation,* compelling traditional hotel chains to reevaluate pricing strategies, services, and customer engagement.

Today, Airbnb stands as one of the most successful disruptors in the travel industry, with a valuation exceeding $100 billion.

Tesla

By reimagining electric vehicles (EVs) and promoting sustainable transportation, Tesla has significantly disrupted both the *automotive and energy* sectors. By delivering high-performance EVs that rival traditional internal combustion engine vehicles in speed, range, and luxury, Tesla reshaped public perception of electric cars.

The company's *Supercharger network* addresses range anxiety, a key barrier to EV adoption, while its *open-source patent strategy* has encouraged other automakers to invest in EV development, accelerating innovation across the industry.

Tesla's advancements in *battery technology, electric drivetrains,* and *autonomous driving* (for example, *Autopilot*) continue to influence both consumer expectations and regulatory landscapes. Its vertically integrated approach and commitment to innovation have not only disrupted incumbent automakers but also spurred global competition in clean energy and sustainable transport.

The Internet

The internet stands as one of the most profound *disruptive innovations* in modern history, fundamentally altering how people communicate, access information, and conduct business. Unlike incremental technological advancements, the internet introduced an entirely new infrastructure for global interconnectedness.

It disrupted industries such as *publishing, retail, entertainment, travel,* and *education* by creating platforms for e-commerce, digital content distribution, online advertising, and remote collaboration. Consumers now wield unprecedented influence through *social media, online reviews, and direct feedback,* reshaping marketing, customer service, and brand engagement.

The internet also democratized access to information, enabled *real-time communication,* and facilitated the emergence of entirely new business models. Its impact continues to evolve, with ripple effects across nearly every sector of society.

Artificial Intelligence (AI)

Transforming industries by automating tasks, AI has enabled personalized experiences and unlocked predictive insights. In finance, AI facilitates algorithmic trading and fraud detection. In healthcare, it powers diagnostic tools, personalized treatment plans, and drug discovery.

AI-enabled *chatbots and virtual assistants* have revolutionized customer service by providing 24/7 support and efficient resolution of routine inquiries. In manufacturing, AI drives operational efficiency by optimizing production schedules, reducing downtime, and enhancing supply chain management.

While AI adoption has led to job displacement in certain sectors (for example, automotive manufacturing), it has simultaneously created new roles in *data science, machine learning,* and *AI system development*. Its ability to *analyze, predict, and personalize* makes AI a powerful disruptive force with long-term implications across nearly all economic domains.

Cryptocurrency

Built on *blockchain technology*, cryptocurrencies offer peer-to-peer transactions, enhanced privacy, and reduced reliance on central banks or intermediaries. *Cryptocurrency*, which particularly decentralizes platforms like Bitcoin and Ethereum, represents a significant potential disruption to the *traditional financial system*.

Cryptocurrencies enable *faster, lower-cost international transfers*, provide financial access to the unbanked, and serve as alternative stores of value and investment assets. They challenge traditional banking structures by *removing gatekeepers*, introducing new forms of capital exchange, and creating decentralized financial ecosystems.

Despite regulatory, scalability, and volatility concerns, cryptocurrencies have already disrupted sectors such as *payments, investing, and fundraising* (for example, via Initial Coin Offerings). Their continued evolution may force traditional financial institutions to innovate and adapt to decentralized models of trust and value transfer.

These case studies demonstrate the power of *disruptive innovation* to reshape industries by targeting overlooked market segments, introducing new business models, and leveraging emerging technologies. Whether through shared mobility, streaming entertainment, peer-to-peer lodging, electric vehicles, or decentralized finance, disruptive innovators continue to challenge the status quo, redefine consumer expectations, and create lasting impact on global economies.

Embracing Disruptive Innovation

More than a technological breakthrough, disruptive innovation is a transformative force that redefines industries through accessibility, affordability, and enhanced user experiences. It challenges long-standing conventions and opens doors to entirely new markets by meeting the needs of underserved or overlooked customers.

As demonstrated by companies like Uber, Netflix, Airbnb, Tesla, and others, disruptive innovation empowers both startups and established enterprises to rethink traditional business models, respond to evolving consumer expectations, and drive sustainable growth. Success in this dynamic landscape requires more than just innovative ideas—it demands bold leadership, organizational agility, and a willingness to take calculated risks.

Businesses that cultivate a culture of innovation and embrace disruption as an opportunity, rather than a threat, are better positioned to lead in an ever-changing world. Whether you're launching a new venture or striving to future-proof a legacy enterprise, understanding and leveraging the principles of disruptive innovation is not just beneficial. It is essential for long-term relevance and success.

11

The Future of Artificial Intelligence

Once confined to the realm of science fiction and academic speculation, artificial intelligence (AI) has evolved into a transformative force shaping every facet of modern life. Once primarily the concern of scientists and mathematicians, AI is now influencing industries, economies, and societies in ways previously unimaginable.

What is AI?

AI is a broad interdisciplinary field focused on creating systems—also known as intelligent agents—that can perceive their environment, make decisions, and perform tasks to achieve specific goals. These systems mimic human cognitive functions such as learning, reasoning, problem-solving, and creativity. Underlying AI technologies include machine learning, deep

> AI is a broad interdisciplinary field focused on creating systems—also known as intelligent agents—that can perceive their environment, make decisions, and perform tasks to achieve specific goals.

learning, and natural language processing. Today's applications fall under the category of Narrow AI, which means they are designed to perform specific tasks with high proficiency, though they lack the general reasoning capabilities of human intelligence.

Examples of AI applications include:

- Autonomous vehicles
- Virtual assistants (for example, Siri, Alexa)
- Customer service chatbots
- AI-driven analytics and recommendation engines

A Brief History

AI's evolution has been marked by a series of groundbreaking milestones. In 1951, Christopher Strachey's checkers program became the first successful AI software to run a complete game on the Ferranti Mark I. Decades later, in 1997, IBM's Deep Blue defeated world chess champion Garry Kasparov, and in 2011, IBM Watson triumphed on *Jeopardy!*, showcasing the power of machine learning and natural language processing.

More recently, OpenAI launched its first Generative Pre-trained Transformer (GPT) model in 2018, leading to the development of ChatGPT and the powerful GPT-4 architecture. These systems can now generate coherent text, images, audio, and other content formats in response to human prompts—ushering in the generative AI era.

Toward General and Super Intelligence

While current AI systems are task-specific, future developments are aimed at achieving Artificial General Intelligence (AGI). AI that can perform any intellectual task a human can. Beyond that, Artificial Superintelligence (ASI) could one day surpass human capabilities altogether. As AI systems continue to advance, their influence will deepen across sectors and geographies.

AI Today: Applications Across Industries

AI is transforming virtually every major industry:

- *Manufacturing*: Robotics and AI-powered sensors enable predictive maintenance, efficient production, and human-machine collaboration.
- *Transportation*: Autonomous vehicles, logistics optimization, and smart traffic management are reshaping mobility.
- *Healthcare*: AI is revolutionizing diagnostics, drug discovery, personalized medicine, and patient monitoring. Algorithms now interpret medical imaging with accuracy rates rivaling or exceeding those of human specialists.
- *Education*: AI enables personalized learning, automated grading, and emotional recognition, allowing educators to tailor lessons to student needs while reducing administrative workload.
- *Finance*: Banks and insurers use AI to detect fraud, assess risk, automate transactions, and analyze investment strategies.
- *Agriculture*: AI-driven robots improve efficiency in crop monitoring, harvesting, and sustainable resource use.
- *Retail and E-commerce*: AI personalizes shopping experiences through predictive analytics and real-time product recommendations.
- *Business Models*: AI is creating entirely new service paradigms, improving operational efficiency, and enabling data-driven decision-making.

Types of AI by Capability

AI systems can be categorized based on their level of sophistication:

- *Narrow AI*: Performs specific tasks (for example, facial recognition, language translation).
- *General AI*: A still theoretical system capable of performing any intellectual task that a human can.
- *Reactive Machines*: Operate on real-time inputs without memory of past experiences.
- *Limited Memory AI*: Uses historical data to inform decisions (for example, self-driving cars).
- *Self-Aware AI*: A hypothetical AI with consciousness and self-awareness.

Challenges and Considerations

As AI adoption accelerates, several critical challenges must be addressed:

Job Displacement and Workforce Transition

AI-driven automation raises concerns about employment. While certain roles, particularly repetitive or administrative ones, may be phased out, AI also creates new opportunities in data science, machine learning, cybersecurity, and AI ethics. Historical resistance to technological change—such as farmers opposing tractors or clerical workers fearing computers—illustrates a pattern of anxiety that ultimately leads to workforce transformation rather than extinction.

Bias and Inequality

AI systems trained on biased data may reinforce societal inequalities. For instance, facial recognition technologies have shown discrepancies in accuracy across different skin tones. To ensure equitable outcomes, developers must proactively identify and eliminate embedded biases in algorithms.

Ethical Concerns

Issues related to fairness, accountability, and transparency in AI decision-making are increasingly under scrutiny. Ethical dilemmas such as AI-generated misinformation, surveillance, and data misuse call for urgent regulation and responsible development practices.

Privacy and Data Use

AI systems require vast datasets to train effectively. This raises significant concerns around data privacy, ownership, and consent. Regulatory bodies like the Federal Trade Commission (FTC) are actively investigating data collection practices by AI companies, emphasizing the need for transparency and user protections.

Regulation and Intellectual Property

Ongoing legal debates—such as copyright lawsuits involving AI-generated content—are prompting a reevaluation of existing laws. Policymakers are under pressure to develop frameworks that balance innovation with consumer rights and intellectual property protections.

Environmental Impact

AI development, particularly training large models, consumes significant energy and resources. While AI has the potential to enhance sustainability (for example, optimizing supply chains), it must be implemented responsibly to avoid exacerbating climate change.

Continuous Learning

The rise of AI necessitates lifelong learning and skill development. Workers, educators, and leaders must continually adapt to emerging technologies to remain competitive in an evolving job landscape.

Quantum Computing and AI Synergy

Quantum computing, still in its nascent stages, could dramatically enhance AI capabilities by exponentially increasing computational power—opening new frontiers in problem-solving and data analysis.

Moving Forward with AI

AI is no longer a futuristic concept—it is an integral part of our present and will define our future. From transforming how we work to reshaping education, healthcare, and communication, AI's potential is vast. However, with this potential comes responsibility.

To harness the benefits while mitigating risks, we must:

- Embrace innovation while fostering ethical AI development.
- Promote inclusive policies to ensure equitable access and opportunity.
- Invest in education and workforce reskilling to prepare for the jobs of tomorrow.

The future of AI will be defined not only by its technological advancements but by our collective ability to guide its development for the greater good. By fostering a balanced, informed, and ethical approach, we can ensure AI serves as a force for progress—creating a more efficient, equitable, and human-centered world.

AI Tomorrow and Beyond

The future of AI envisions a world where intelligent systems are deeply embedded in our daily lives—automating tasks, enhancing decision-making, and transforming industries. AI is expected to become increasingly ubiquitous, shaping how we work, learn, communicate, and interact with technology. While this integration promises substantial benefits such as improved efficiency and innovation, it also raises important concerns, including workforce displacement, data privacy, ethical dilemmas, and regulatory challenges.

The Path to the Future

AI is evolving at a rapid pace and is poised to have a profound impact on society in the near future. Its continued development will be influenced by technological breakthroughs, increased global investment, and shifting societal attitudes toward automation and digital transformation.

Currently, an estimated 55 percent of organizations have adopted AI in some form—an indication of its accelerating integration across industries. In the coming years, we can expect AI to become more user-friendly and accessible, empowering individuals and businesses alike to leverage its capabilities regardless of technical expertise.

Key Developments and Trends

Enhanced Integration into Daily Life

AI will become more ingrained in everyday activities through smart assistants, autonomous devices, personalized digital services, and intelligent automation. Collaborative AI systems will increasingly work alongside humans to support productivity and decision-making, leading to more human-centric work environments.

Accelerated Decision-Making

AI's ability to analyze massive datasets and convert findings into intuitive visual insights will expedite decision-making across sectors. Business leaders will rely less on manual data analysis and more on real-time, AI-driven insights to guide strategy and operations.

Economic Growth and Productivity

AI will serve as a catalyst for economic growth by creating new products, services, and markets. Intelligent automation will increase labor productivity by optimizing repetitive tasks, while also enabling the emergence of a "virtual workforce" capable of autonomous problem-solving and continuous learning.

Sector-specific Impacts

Transportation

Autonomous vehicles will become more prevalent in both consumer and commercial applications. From self-driving cars on highways to robotic spacecraft ferrying cargo and astronauts, transportation is expected to be one of the most visible indicators of our arrival in the AI age.

Workplace Transformation

AI will automate routine tasks, augment human decision-making, and foster more adaptive workflows. AI agents capable of completing complex tasks—beyond simply answering questions—will become commonplace, functioning as virtual coworkers. This shift will demand employee upskilling and changes in workforce structure.

Job Market and Employment

AI may impact up to 40 percent of jobs globally. While many existing roles may be displaced, the technology will also create new opportunities in emerging fields such as AI engineering, robotics, data science, and user experience design. The overall effect will be a significant transformation rather than a net loss of employment.

Healthcare

AI will become a core component of diagnostic and clinical decision-making, improving the accuracy and speed of diagnoses. However, the increasing reliance on AI in healthcare will raise legal, ethical, and data privacy challenges. Navigating patient rights, data ownership, and compliance will become more complex and expensive.

Education

AI will personalize learning experiences by adapting educational content to each student's needs and learning style. From primary to higher education, AI-powered platforms will help optimize teaching strategies, enhance student engagement, and improve outcomes.

Finance

AI algorithms already influence stock trading, portfolio management, and fraud detection. In the future, financial institutions will use AI to perform high-frequency trading, predict market trends, assess credit risk, and ensure regulatory compliance—potentially outperforming human analysts in accuracy and speed.

Marketing and Advertising

AI will drive hyper-personalized advertising by analyzing individual behaviors, preferences, and contexts. Businesses are increasingly testing AI in marketing to improve targeting, customer engagement, and conversion rates.

Communication

AI will revolutionize communication by understanding nuances beyond literal meanings and enhancing accessibility for individuals with disabilities. Advanced conversational agents will facilitate seamless dialogue across languages, cultures, and contexts—supporting global collaboration and inclusive interaction.

Military and Cybersecurity

AI will play a pivotal role in developing autonomous defense systems, surveillance tools, and cyber threat-prevention technologies. While enhancing national security, these applications will also demand new ethical frameworks and oversight mechanisms to prevent misuse.

Law and Legal Services

Small legal teams equipped with AI tools will perform tasks traditionally requiring larger staffs, dramatically improving efficiency and lowering costs. The legal industry may see a significant reduction in the number of practicing attorneys, especially in document-intensive roles, as AI assumes greater responsibility in case analysis, contract review, and legal research.

Risks and Ethical Concerns

While the promise of AI is vast, its responsible development and deployment are critical. Key concerns include:

- *Privacy and Data Ownership*: The use of personal data to train AI models raises questions about consent, transparency, and data governance.
- *Algorithmic Bias*: AI systems trained on biased data risk perpetuating or even amplifying societal inequities.
- *Security Threats*: In the wrong hands, AI could be weaponized—used to conduct cyberattacks, disseminate misinformation, or deploy autonomous weapons.
- *Loss of Control*: As AI systems grow more complex, their decision-making processes may become opaque, raising fears about the ability to explain and human oversight.
- *Technological Singularity*: Some theorists warn of a scenario in which AI surpasses human intelligence, potentially leading to unintended consequences or existential risks if left unchecked.

A Balanced Perspective

AI is rapidly becoming a foundational element of modern society. From helping elderly individuals live independently to enabling real-time language translation, AI holds extraordinary potential to improve quality of life, enhance productivity, and foster global innovation.

However, the narrative of AI is not one of machines taking over the world. Rather, it is about reimagining how work gets done, how services are delivered, and how humans and machines can collaborate more effectively. At the heart of this evolution is the rise of intelligent agents—AI systems capable of learning, adapting, and acting autonomously.

As we move forward, the outcome of the AI revolution will depend largely on how we choose to guide its development. By investing in ethical frameworks, transparent governance, education, and human-centered design, we can ensure that AI contributes positively to society—minimizing risks while maximizing its transformative benefits.

The question is not whether AI will shape the future, but how we will shape the future of AI.

12

Starting Your Own Business

Small and middle-sized businesses are the backbone of the US economy. Together, they account for over 40 percent of the nation's Gross Domestic Product (GDP). Small businesses alone comprise approximately 95 percent of all US enterprises and employ nearly 45 percent of the private workforce. Yet, despite their critical role, many of these ventures fail to achieve their full potential—often due to limited access to coaching, capital, connections, and curriculum. Bridging these gaps is essential for empowering entrepreneurs to scale their businesses and achieve long-term success.

Embarking on the journey of entrepreneurship is exciting and full of promise. You may have innovative ideas and ambitious goals, but the path to building a successful business is rarely straightforward. Each entrepreneur faces a unique set of challenges and decisions, from ideation to execution. This chapter provides a comprehensive roadmap to help you navigate the process of launching and sustaining your own business, covering everything from developing

> You may have innovative ideas and ambitious goals, but the path to building a successful business is rarely straightforward.

your concept to legally establishing your company and securing funding.

Developing a Business Idea

Every successful business starts with a solid idea—one that solves a real-world problem or fulfills an unmet need. Begin by identifying pain points, inefficiencies, or gaps in the market that you can address. Once you've generated an idea, refine it through research and customer feedback to establish a clear value proposition.

If you don't have a specific concept in mind, consider starting with service-oriented businesses that require lower capital investment, such as:

- Business consulting
- Freelance writing or graphic design
- Event or financial planning
- Computer training or IT support
- Personal training, photography, or book-keeping
- Jewelry design or interior decoration

Conducting Market Research

Before investing time and money, evaluate whether your idea has commercial viability. Market research allows you to assess customer demand, competitive dynamics, and industry trends. Key steps include:

- Identifying your target market: Define who your ideal customers are based on demographics, behavior, and needs.
- Analyzing competitors: Understand their offerings, pricing, customer reviews, and potential gaps in the market.

- Engaging your audience: Use surveys, interviews, and focus groups to gain insights and validate assumptions.

Benefits of market research include:

- Understanding customer needs
- Identifying potential obstacles
- Reducing financial risk
- Uncovering untapped market niches
- Setting informed business goals

Creating a Business Plan

Your business plan serves as the blueprint for launching and growing your company. It outlines your goals, strategies, and operational structure. A strong business plan helps you:

- Clarify your vision and strategy
- Communicate with potential investors or partners
- Identify risks and prepare for challenges
- Organize your team and operations

A comprehensive business plan typically includes:

- Executive summary
- Market and competitive analysis
- Marketing and sales strategy
- Operational plan
- Financial projections
- Funding requirements

Resources such as the US Small Business Administration (SBA) offer templates and guidance for writing an effective business plan.

Choosing a Business Structure

Selecting the right legal structure is a critical decision with tax, liability, and regulatory implications. Common options include:

- *Sole Proprietorship*: Simplest form; owner-controlled but personally liable.
- *Limited Liability Company (LLC)*: Provides liability protection with flexible management.
- *Partnership (Limited Partner [LP]/Limited Liability Partnership [LLP])*: Involves two or more owners; shared responsibilities and profits.
- *Corporation (C-Corp/S-Corp*—the distinguishing features between C/Corp vs. S/Corp are related to taxation and flexibility of ownership*)*: Offers limited liability and access to capital but requires more regulatory compliance.

Consulting a legal or tax advisor can help you choose the structure that best aligns with your goals and risk-tolerance.

Estimating Startup Costs

There is no universal amount required to start a business—costs vary depending on your industry and business model. However, you can estimate your needs by evaluating:

- *Capital Expenditures*: One-time costs for furniture, equipment, technology, and inventory.

- *Operating Expenses*: Ongoing costs such as salaries, rent, utilities, and marketing.
- *Existing Assets*: Include personal savings, pre-owned equipment, or available space.

Answering key questions about initial and ongoing expenses will help you plan more effectively and avoid cash flow issues.

Securing Funding

Access to capital is essential, yet 38 percent of small businesses fail due to funding shortages. Your business plan will clarify how much capital you need and support your case when seeking funding. Potential funding sources include:

- Personal savings or credit
- Family and friends
- Bank or SBA loans
- Angel investors or venture capital
- Local grants and economic development programs
- Crowdfunding platforms

Your legal structure, industry, and background may influence your funding options. For example, minority-, women-, or veteran-owned businesses may be eligible for specialized grants and loans.

Selecting a Business Location

Your location—physical or digital—can significantly impact your success. Consider:

- Visibility and accessibility
- Tax implications and local regulations
- Proximity to suppliers and customers

For online businesses, choose a reliable e-commerce platform and ensure that your website is user-friendly and secure.

Naming and Registering Your Business

Choose a business name that is memorable, reflects your brand identity, and has an available domain. Once chosen:

- Reserve your name with your state's business registry (if needed)
- Register with the appropriate state and federal authorities
- Apply for a federal Employer Identification Number (EIN)

Legal and Financial Compliance

To operate legally, you may need to:

- Obtain local, state, and federal licenses or permits
- Open a business checking account
- Understand your tax obligations and register for state/federal taxes
- Establish accounting, payroll, and book-keeping systems

Consulting legal and financial professionals is highly recommended during this phase to ensure compliance and long-term stability.

Insuring Your Business

Protect your venture with the appropriate types of insurance:

- *General Liability*: Covers bodily injury, property damage, and legal claims.
- *Professional Liability*: Protects against negligence or errors in service delivery.
- *Commercial Property*: Covers damage to physical assets like inventory and equipment.
- *Business Income Insurance*: Compensates for lost income due to unforeseen closures.

Some insurance types, such as workers' compensation, may be legally required in your state.

Obtaining Licenses and Permits

Certain businesses require specialized licenses or permits, often at multiple levels of government. Examples include:

- Food service licenses
- Alcohol permits
- Zoning approvals
- Environmental clearances

Seek legal counsel to identify and satisfy all applicable regulatory requirements for your business type and location.

Building Your Brand and Online Presence

A strong brand and digital footprint are essential for success. This includes:

- Developing a brand identity (name, logo, messaging)
- Creating a website and social media profiles
- Building a customer email list for direct communication
- Launching marketing campaigns to build awareness and drive sales

Operating and Managing Your Business

Once operational, focus on efficient management and continuous improvement:

- Implement systems for inventory, Human Resources (HR), accounting, and customer service
- Monitor business performance using Key Performance Indicators (KPIs)
- Manage risks through insurance and compliance
- Plan for expansion based on demand and market conditions

Seeking Expert Guidance

First-time entrepreneurs often benefit from external support. Consider:

- *Mentors*: Seasoned professionals who provide strategic advice and support

- *Outside Advisors*: Experts in law, finance, marketing, or operations
- *Startup Attorneys*: Legal professionals with experience in launching new ventures
- *SBA and Nonprofit Resources*: Free or low-cost mentoring, training, and business counseling

The most valuable advisors understand both your industry and the startup environment, offering insights that go beyond technical expertise to guide your business holistically.

Launching Your Business

Congratulations—your business is ready to launch! Celebrate your progress, but also stay focused on what comes next: building your customer base, managing operations, refining your strategies, and preparing for growth.

Starting a business is a significant milestone, one that demands resilience, adaptability, and continuous learning. With the right planning, support, and determination, your entrepreneurial journey can lead to a thriving and impactful enterprise.

13

Rags to Riches

Entrepreneurial Stories

Tip for Readers: *Don't just read these stories—use them as a mirror. Your journey may not look the same, but every great entrepreneur starts with limited means, an obstacle to overcome, and a vision that others cannot yet see.*

Many successful entrepreneurs have achieved immense wealth despite starting from humble beginnings. These individuals overcame significant challenges, such as poverty, homelessness, and the lack of opportunity, to build successful businesses and achieve financial independence. These "rags to riches" stories often highlight the power of hard work, perseverance, and taking calculated risks.

The Entrepreneurial Journey of Benjamin Franklin

Benjamin Franklin's life remains one of the most iconic stories in American history. From humble beginnings to lasting prominence, Franklin's rise is not merely a tale of wealth accumulation but a blueprint for personal growth, innovation, and civic impact. His entrepreneurial journey exemplifies the power of self-education, industriousness, and purpose-driven ambition.

Humble Beginnings and Early Hunger for Knowledge

Born in 1706 in Boston, Massachusetts, Benjamin Franklin was the 15th of 17 children. His father, Josiah Franklin, earned a modest living as a candle and soap maker. With limited financial means, Benjamin's formal education was cut short after only two years. Despite this, he developed a voracious appetite for learning, educating himself through books and self-directed study. This early commitment to knowledge would become a cornerstone of his future success.

Apprenticeship and the Printing Trade

At the age of 12, Franklin became an apprentice to his older brother James, a printer. This opportunity introduced him to the world of publishing and the persuasive power of the written word. Although their relationship was strained, Franklin managed to publish a series of satirical essays under the pseudonym *Silence Dogood*, revealing his talent for wit and commentary. Seeking independence and a new beginning, he ran away to Philadelphia at 17, arriving with little money but immense ambition.

Building a Printing Empire

In Philadelphia, Franklin's reputation as a skilled and reliable printer grew steadily. A brief period working in London enhanced his technical expertise, and upon returning to Philadelphia, he launched his own printing business. His big break came when he secured the contract to serve as the official printer for the Pennsylvania government. This steady income allowed him to invest in further ventures, most notably the publication of *Poor Richard's Almanack*. Blending humor, wisdom, and practical advice, the almanac achieved wide circulation and solidified Franklin's status as a successful entrepreneur.

Expanding Through Innovation and Scale

Franklin's approach to entrepreneurship was forward-thinking and scalable. He trained apprentices and formed partnerships across the colonies, essentially pioneering one of the first franchised business models in America. He also diversified his investments—acquiring real estate, co-owning a paper mill, and expanding into other commercial ventures. His strategic thinking and resource management reflect a deep understanding of business fundamentals, long before modern theories of entrepreneurship were articulated.

Civic Entrepreneurship and Public Impact

Beyond his financial accomplishments, Franklin was deeply committed to public service and societal improvement. He helped found America's first public library, the University of Pennsylvania, and the first volunteer fire department in Philadelphia. His entrepreneurial mindset extended into public initiatives, demonstrating how business success can be a platform for civic innovation. These contributions enhanced not only his own legacy but also the infrastructure and educational opportunities of early American society.

Legacy of a True Entrepreneur

Benjamin Franklin's story transcends wealth. It is a powerful narrative of self-determination, intellectual growth, and the use of success to improve one's community. From a boy with limited means to a statesman, inventor, and Founding Father, Franklin's life reflects the enduring values of curiosity, hard work, and public purpose.

A Life of Lasting Value

Franklin's entrepreneurial journey is a timeless lesson in how determination, education, and innovation can turn adversity into achievement. His life illustrates that true success is not defined by wealth alone, but by the positive impact one creates. Franklin remains a symbol of the American Dream—proof that with vision, discipline, and service to others, it is possible to rise from obscurity to greatness and leave a legacy that inspires generations to come.

Oprah Winfrey: From Poverty to Power

Oprah Winfrey's extraordinary rise from poverty and trauma to global influence is one of the most compelling entrepreneurial stories of our time. Her path was neither smooth nor conventional, but it was paved with resilience, authenticity, and strategic vision. Oprah's life exemplifies the power of owning one's narrative and turning adversity into achievement.

Early Life: Hardship and Adversity

Born on January 29, 1954, in rural Mississippi to a single teenage mother, Oprah Gail Winfrey faced overwhelming odds from the beginning. Raised in deep poverty, she often wore potato sacks as clothing due to her family's inability to afford proper garments. Her childhood was marked by instability and repeated abuse. At just 13 years old, she ran away from home, and by 14, she had given birth to a son who died in infancy. These early traumas could have derailed her future—but they did not define her.

Discovering Her Voice

Despite these hardships, Oprah demonstrated a remarkable talent for public speaking, which earned her a scholarship to Tennessee State University after winning a speech contest. This opened the door to the world of media. At 19, she became the youngest and first Black female news anchor at WLAC-TV in Nashville. However, her career took a detour when she was demoted from a news anchor's role in Baltimore. Rather than giving up, Oprah transitioned to daytime television—a genre that would soon launch her to national fame.

Breakthrough in Television

In 1984, Oprah was offered the opportunity to host a low-rated morning talk show in Chicago called *AM Chicago*. Within months, her empathetic and relatable communication style transformed the program, catapulting it to the top of the ratings. By 1986, the show went national and was renamed *The Oprah Winfrey Show*. Unlike typical talk shows of the time, Oprah's content focused on real-life struggles, emotional well-being, and personal development—topics that deeply resonated with viewers and set her apart from the competition.

Building a Media Empire

The pivotal moment in Oprah's entrepreneurial journey came in 1988 when she founded *Harpo Productions*—"Oprah" spelled backwards. This move granted her complete creative and financial control over her work, an unprecedented step for a media personality at the time. Under Harpo, she expanded her reach by producing films, television specials, and launching *O, The Oprah Magazine*. Oprah's entrepreneurial strategy was rooted in ownership, authenticity, and a commitment to empowering others.

Expanding the Brand and Giving Back

Oprah continued to grow her brand with the launch of the *Oprah Winfrey Network (OWN)* in 2011, a channel dedicated to inspirational and uplifting content. She also made strategic business investments, including a notable stake in *Weight Watchers*, and entered a content partnership with *Apple TV+*. Beyond her business ventures, Oprah's philanthropic efforts have been profound. She founded the *Oprah Winfrey Leadership Academy for Girls* in South Africa, providing educational opportunities to underserved communities and reinforcing her lifelong commitment to empowerment through education.

A Legacy of Influence and Empowerment

Today, Oprah Winfrey is not only a billionaire—with a net worth exceeding $2.5 billion—but a global symbol of perseverance, leadership, and transformative entrepreneurship. Her journey from severe hardship to becoming one of the most influential figures in media proves that setbacks are not endpoints but opportunities for redirection. Oprah didn't just build a brand—she built a movement rooted in empathy, empowerment, and personal growth.

More Than a Success Story

Oprah Winfrey's life is far more than a rags to riches tale—it is a masterclass in visionary entrepreneurship. Through resilience, authenticity, and a relentless pursuit of purpose, she redefined what it means to be a media mogul. Her journey teaches us that no obstacle is insurmountable when met with courage and clarity of vision. Oprah's legacy is not only measured in wealth and influence but in the lives she has touched and the example she continues to set for aspiring entrepreneurs around the world.

Walt Disney: From Penniless Dreamer to Entertainment Visionary

Walt Disney's rise from being a struggling artist to become the founder of one of the world's most powerful entertainment companies is a remarkable story of resilience, innovation, and unshakable vision. His journey is not merely a rags to riches tale—it is a celebration of creativity, perseverance, and the enduring power of dreaming big.

Humble Beginnings and Artistic Ambition

Born on December 5, 1901, in Chicago, Illinois, Walt Disney was raised in a modest household. His father, Elias Disney, was a stern man who struggled to succeed in various business ventures, forcing the family to relocate frequently. From a young age, Walt showed a passion for drawing and storytelling, but financial hardship limited his access to formal artistic training. Despite the challenges, his creative spark never dimmed.

Early Failures and Lessons in Resilience

After briefly serving as an ambulance driver during World War I, Disney launched his first animation studio, Laugh-O-Gram, in Kansas City. The studio produced short films based on classic fairy tales but quickly went bankrupt due to financial mismanagement and unreliable clients. Undeterred, Disney took a bold leap and moved to Hollywood in 1923 with just $40 in his pocket, hoping to find greater opportunity in the booming film industry.

Building a Studio and Bouncing Back

In Hollywood, Walt joined forces with his brother Roy to establish the *Disney Brothers Studio*. Their first major success came with the creation of *Oswald the Lucky Rabbit*, but disaster struck when Walt lost the rights to the character in a contractual dispute. Most of his animators were also lured away by competitors, leaving the fledgling studio on the brink of collapse once again.

Rather than accept defeat, Disney responded with resilience and originality. He created a new character—*Mickey Mouse*—who debuted in the 1928 cartoon *Steamboat Willie*, one of the first animations to feature synchronized sound. Mickey Mouse became an instant sensation, propelling the Disney studio into national prominence.

Revolutionizing Animation

Following the success of Mickey Mouse, Disney continued to push creative boundaries. In 1937, he released *Snow White and the Seven Dwarfs*, the first-ever full-length animated feature film. Despite industry skepticism—critics dubbed the project as "Disney's Folly"—the film earned over $8 million during the Great Depression, a monumental success that proved animation could be both artistically and commercially viable. This marked the beginning of a new era in cinematic storytelling.

Bringing Dreams to Life: The Creation of Disneyland

Never content to limit his imagination to the screen, Walt Disney envisioned a place where families could immerse themselves in magical worlds. That vision materialized with the opening of *Disneyland* in Anaheim, California, in 1955. Unlike traditional amusement parks, Disneyland offered themed experiences based on beloved characters and stories. Although initially met with skepticism and financial risk, the park was an overwhelming success and became a model for themed entertainment around the world.

Lasting Legacy and Global Impact

Walt Disney passed away in 1966, but his legacy lives on through *The Walt Disney Company*, a global entertainment conglomerate encompassing film, television, theme parks, merchandise, and more. His innovations revolutionized not only animation but also the way audiences experience storytelling. His relentless pursuit of excellence and creativity made him one of the most influential entrepreneurs of the 20th century.

The Courage to Dream Big

Walt Disney's life is a powerful reminder that success is not defined by one's beginnings, but by the persistence to overcome failure and the courage to implement dreams boldly. From bankruptcy and setbacks to iconic achievements and global influence, Disney's entrepreneurial journey exemplifies how vision, resilience, and creativity can transform challenges into triumphs. As he famously said, *"All our dreams can come true, if we have the courage to pursue them."* Walt Disney didn't just pursue his dreams—he invited the world to dream with him.

Sam Walton: Fulfilling the American Dream

The American Dream is built on the foundation that anyone, regardless of background, can achieve greatness through hard work, perseverance, and innovation. Few embody this ideal as completely as Sam Walton, the founder of Walmart. From humble beginnings during the Great Depression to establishing one of the most successful retail empires in history, Walton's story is a classic example of grit, vision, and entrepreneurial brilliance.

Humble Beginnings

Born on March 29, 1918, in Kingfisher, Oklahoma, Sam Walton grew up during one of the most challenging periods in American history—the Great Depression. His family was of modest means, and they struggled to make ends meet. From a young age, Sam demonstrated a strong work ethic. He worked various odd jobs, including delivering newspapers and selling magazine subscriptions, to help support his family. These early experiences taught him the value of money, customer service, and hard work.

The Spark of Entrepreneurship

After graduating from the University of Missouri with a degree in economics in 1940, Walton began working for J.C. Penney as a management trainee. His experience there laid the foundation for his understanding of the retail business. Following a stint in the military during World War II, Walton used a $20,000 loan from his father-in-law and $5,000 of his own savings to purchase a Ben Franklin variety store in Newport, Arkansas.

Sam's first major success came from his ability to innovate and take calculated risks. He focused on offering lower prices by negotiating better deals with suppliers and improving inventory management—principles that would later become the core of Walmart's business model.

The Birth of Walmart

After losing the lease on his original store in 1950, Walton relocated to Bentonville, Arkansas, where he opened Walton's Five and Dime. Over the next decade, he continued to refine his retail strategy, focusing on small towns that were often neglected by larger retailers. He saw an opportunity where others saw a risk: delivering low prices and high value to rural America.

In 1962, Sam Walton opened the first Walmart in Rogers, Arkansas. His core philosophy was simple: "*Give customers what they want at a lower price and they'll keep coming back.*" By leveraging a cost-cutting approach, high-volume sales, and efficient supply chain management, Walton revolutionized the retail industry.

A Retail Empire

Under Walton's leadership, Walmart grew at an unprecedented rate. By the 1980s, Walmart had become one of the largest retailers in the US. Walton was known for his hands-on management style, commitment to employee involvement, and relentless focus on efficiency. He introduced concepts like profit-sharing with employees and encouraged a culture of thrift and customer-focus.

In 1985, Sam Walton was named the richest man in America by *Forbes* magazine. Yet, he remained modest in his lifestyle and stayed true to his values. He famously drove a pickup truck and wore inexpensive clothes, reflecting his belief in humility and simplicity.

Legacy

Sam Walton passed away in 1992, but his legacy lives on. Today, Walmart is a global retail powerhouse, operating thousands of stores across the world. Walton's approach to business has influenced generations of entrepreneurs and transformed the landscape of retail.

More than just a businessman, Sam Walton was a visionary who proved that innovation, integrity, and determination can overcome even the most difficult of beginnings. His journey from a small-town boy during the Great Depression to the founder of a multibillion-dollar enterprise is a testament to the power of the entrepreneurial spirit.

J.K. Rowling: From Welfare to Worldwide Phenomenon

In her journey from a struggling single mother to the creator of a global literary and media empire, J.K. Rowling is one of the most compelling examples of resilience, imagination, and entrepreneurial vision. Her story underscores the power of perseverance in the face of adversity and the transformative potential of a single idea.

A Passion for Writing from an Early Age

Joanne Rowling was born in 1965 in England. From a young age, she showed a deep love for storytelling, writing her first story at the age of six. Despite her early passion, Rowling's path to becoming a published author was long and difficult.

Hardship and Personal Struggles

In the early 1990s, Rowling's life reached a low point. After studying French and classics at the University of Exeter, she worked as a researcher and bilingual secretary for Amnesty International. She later moved to Portugal to teach English, where she married and had a daughter, Jessica. The marriage ended in divorce after a little over a year, marked by emotional distress.

Returning to the UK, Rowling settled in Edinburgh with her infant daughter. Unemployed, living on government assistance, and battling severe depression, she often wrote in cafes while Jessica slept. Rowling has since revealed that her experiences with depression inspired the terrifying Dementors in the *Harry Potter* series.

The Birth of Harry Potter

The idea for *Harry Potter* came to Rowling during a delayed train ride from Manchester to London in 1990. She envisioned a young boy who discovers he is a wizard and attends a secret school of magic. The concept gripped her imagination, and she began writing what would become Harry Potter and the Philosopher's Stone.

Over several years, Rowling handwrote the manuscript in cafes, with limited resources and no computer. She persevered through exhaustion and discouragement, driven by a belief in her story.

Rejection and Breakthrough

Rowling submitted the manuscript to numerous publishers—12 rejected it. Many believed children wouldn't read a book of that length. Eventually, in 1996, Bloomsbury Publishing took a chance after the chairman's eight-year-old daughter read the first chapter and asked for more.

In 1997, *Harry Potter and the Philosopher's Stone* was published with an initial print run of just 500 copies. It marked the beginning of an unprecedented literary phenomenon.

Building a Global Franchise

The *Harry Potter* series quickly became the best-selling book series in history, translated into over 80 languages and selling more than 500 million copies worldwide. It spawned a billion-dollar film franchise, stage productions, merchandise lines, and theme parks.

What set Rowling apart was not just her creativity but her business acumen. She retained significant creative control over her work, personally reviewing scripts, licensing deals, and product lines. She established *Pottermore* (now *Wizarding World*), a digital platform for content and fan engagement, demonstrating her understanding of brand management in the digital age

Expansion and Philanthropy

Rowling continued expanding the magical universe with the *Fantastic Beasts* film series and *Harry Potter and the Cursed Child*, a successful stage production. Her ventures extended beyond books, proving she was more than an author—she was an entrepreneurial force.

Despite amassing the status of a billionaire, Rowling became one of the most charitable figures in the UK. Through her foundation, *Lumos*, and other philanthropic efforts, she has donated hundreds of millions to causes focused on children, healthcare, and social justice. She notably dropped off *Forbes*' billionaire list due to her extensive charitable giving.

A Story of Vision, Grit, and Empowerment

J.K. Rowling's journey is a powerful narrative of triumph over adversity. From poverty and rejection to global fame and business success, she exemplifies how vision, grit, and authenticity can turn a single idea into a transformative legacy. Her story reminds us that even in the darkest times, belief in your purpose—combined with resilience and creativity—can illuminate the world.

Lucy Guo: From Teen Hustler to America's Youngest Self-Made Female Billionaire

Overview

Lucy Guo, aged 30, has recently been recognized as the world's youngest self-made female billionaire, surpassing Taylor Swift, the famous singer.

Humble Beginnings

Raised in Fremont, California by Chinese immigrant parents who worked as electrical engineers, Lucy Guo showed entrepreneurial flair early—trading Pokémon cards, flipping online game assets, and coding bots well before her high school years.

The Turning Point: Scale AI

Guo dropped out of Carnegie Mellon University after receiving a $100K Thiel Fellowship. She co-founded *Scale AI* in 2016, and although she left the company in 2018, she retained a roughly 5 *per cent equity stake*. As Scale AI's valuation soared to around $25 billion, her stake became worth over *$1.2–1.3 billion*.

New Ventures and Creator Economy

After Scale AI, Guo founded *Backend Capital*, a Venture Capital (VC) firm funding early-stage engineering startups, and in 2022, she launched *Passes*, a creator monetization platform aimed at a more sustainable content model. Passes has raised approximately $40 million and is valued at around $150 million.

Persona and Impact

Despite her wealth, Guo remains known for her frugality and modest lifestyle. She champions women in tech, stresses the importance of timing in entrepreneurship, and emphasizes building stakeholder-focused businesses.

Why Lucy Guo's Story Resonates Today

- *Relatable Beginning*: Growing up in a middle-class immigrant household, Guo's early ventures—like Pokémon card trading—highlight how small initiatives can scale dramatically when paired with talent and timing.
- *Strategic Exit, Lasting Gains*: Though she left Scale AI early, her retained equity made her a billionaire—demonstrating that initial positioning, not just leadership roles, can yield extraordinary outcomes.
- *Creator Economy Focus:* Unlike traditional tech paths, Guo pivoted toward empowering creators through Passes, aligning with emerging trends in digital content monetization.
- *Grounded Persona*: Her down-to-earth public image makes her story especially compelling in an age often marked by glamour and excess.

Narayana Murthy: Founder of Infosys

Humble Beginnings

N.R. Narayana Murthy was born in 1946 in Mysore, Karnataka, India, into a middle-class family. His father was a schoolteacher, and resources were modest. Despite financial limitations, Murthy excelled in academics and earned a degree in electrical engineering from the National Institute of Engineering, followed by a Master's degree from IIT Kanpur.

Struggles and Early Failures

After graduation, Murthy worked at the Indian Institute of Management, Ahmedabad, as a chief systems programmer. Later, he attempted to start a company called *Softronics*, but the venture failed within just 18 months. This failure was discouraging, but he viewed it as a learning experience rather than a setback.

Founding Infosys with $250

In 1981, with just *₹10,000 (about $250 at the time)* borrowed from his wife Sudha Murthy, Narayana Murthy co-founded Infosys along with six colleagues. They had no office space, no infrastructure, and limited funds, but they had a vision: to build a global IT services company from India.

The Turning Point

During the 1980s and 1990s, India's IT outsourcing industry began to grow, and Infosys was at the forefront. They pioneered the *Global Delivery Model*, which became the backbone of India's software services exports. Unlike many businesses at the time, Murthy insisted on *transparency, ethical business practices,* and *employee ownership.*

Rise to Riches

Infosys became the first Indian company to be listed on the NASDAQ in 1999. Murthy, once a man who had to rely on his wife's savings, became a billionaire and a respected global business leader. Today, Infosys is worth *tens of billions of dollars*, employing over 300,000 people worldwide.

Legacy

Narayana Murthy is often called the *"Father of the Indian IT sector"*. Beyond his personal wealth, his story is about building an institution that gave India a respected place in the global technology map. His journey from a modest background to leading one of the world's largest IT companies is a classic rags to riches entrepreneurial tale.

Lakshmi Niwas Mittal: The Steel Tycoon

Humble Beginnings

Lakshmi Mittal was born in 1950 in Sadulpur, Rajasthan, into a Marwari business family with very limited means. His father owned a small steel business in Calcutta (now Kolkata), where the family lived in a modest shared house with no luxuries. Growing up, Mittal experienced firsthand the struggles of scarcity and the determination needed to rise above limitations.

Education and Early Career

Mittal studied commerce at St. Xavier's College, Kolkata. After graduation, he joined his father's modest steel business. At the time, India's restrictive industrial policies made it nearly impossible to expand domestically, so Mittal began looking abroad for opportunities.

First Breakthrough: Indonesia, 1976

At just 26, Mittal ventured out independently and established a steel plant in Indonesia. Starting with almost nothing but courage and ambition, he modernized operations, improved efficiency, and proved his ability to turn struggling plants into profitable businesses.

The "Turnaround King"

Through the 1980s and 1990s, Mittal acquired sick and failing steel plants across the globe—in Trinidad, Mexico, Canada, and Kazakhstan. Each time, he revived them with cost efficiency, lean operations, and aggressive expansion strategies. His philosophy was simple: *buy struggling companies at low cost, restructure them, and make them world-class.*

Rise to Riches

By 2004, Mittal Steel had become the world's largest steelmaker. In 2006, he orchestrated one of the most high-profile corporate takeovers in history by merging with Arcelor to form *ArcelorMittal*, the world's largest steel company. This bold move cemented his status as a global business icon.

Wealth and Recognition

From a boy in a modest household in Rajasthan, Mittal rose to become one of the richest men in the world. In 2005, *Forbes* ranked him as the *third-richest person globally*. He is also known for his philanthropy in education and sports, supporting Indian athletes and institutions.

Legacy

Lakshmi Mittal is widely regarded as the *"Steel King of the World"*. His story reflects resilience, global vision, and the courage to seize opportunities far beyond one's homeland. He transformed a struggling family business into a global steel empire spanning more than 60 countries.

Indra Nooyi: From Chennai to CEO of PepsiCo

Humble Beginnings

Indra Nooyi was born in 1955 in Chennai, India, into a conservative middle-class Tamil family. Her father worked at the State Bank of Hyderabad, and her mother was a homemaker. Despite limited means, her family placed tremendous value on education and discipline. As a girl, she often studied late into the night, using kerosene lamps when electricity failed.

Early Education and Struggles

Nooyi excelled in academics and was also bold enough to step outside traditional expectations. She played cricket in college and even joined a women's rock band as a guitarist. She earned a degree in physics, chemistry, and mathematics from Madras Christian College, followed by an MBA from the Indian Institute of Management (IIM), Calcutta.

Breaking Barriers Abroad

In the late 1970s, Nooyi moved to the US to study at Yale School of Management. Life was tough—she worked night shifts as a receptionist to support herself and often wore a sari to job interviews because she couldn't afford business suits. But her perseverance and brilliance helped her break through cultural and professional barriers.

Climbing the Corporate Ladder

Nooyi's career took off when she joined Boston Consulting Group, followed by leadership roles at Motorola and Asea Brown Boveri. Her sharp strategic thinking, bold decision-making, and ability to simplify complex problems earned her recognition.

The Big Break: PepsiCo, 1994

Nooyi joined PepsiCo in 1994 and quickly rose through the ranks. She was instrumental in major strategic moves, including PepsiCo's acquisition of Tropicana, the merger with Quaker Oats (bringing Gatorade into the portfolio), and the company's pivot toward healthier products.

CEO of PepsiCo, 2006–2018

In 2006, Indra Nooyi became the *CEO of PepsiCo*, one of the largest food and beverage companies in the world, and one of the very few women—and women of color—leading a Fortune 500 company at the time. Under her leadership, PepsiCo's revenues grew from $35 billion to $63.5 billion.

Legacy and Recognition

Nooyi is consistently ranked among the world's most powerful women by *Forbes* and *Fortune*. She broke glass ceilings for women and people of Indian origin globally, all while staying deeply connected to her roots. She often credits her success to her upbringing in Chennai, where humility, discipline, and persistence were instilled in her from childhood.

In Her Own Words

Nooyi once said: *"Just because you are CEO, don't think you have landed. You must continually increase your learning, the way you think, and the way you approach the organization."*

Sundar Pichai: From Chennai to CEO of Google and Alphabet

Humble Beginnings

Pichai Sundararajan, known as Sundar Pichai, was born in 1972 in Madurai, Tamil Nadu, and grew up in a modest two-room apartment in Chennai. His father was an electrical engineer at General Electric Company (GEC), and his mother was a stenographer. The family lived without luxuries—no car, no television, and for a long time, no telephone.

Early Spark of Curiosity

As a child, Pichai displayed an extraordinary memory, especially with numbers. He could remember every phone number dialed on the family's first landline telephone. Despite financial constraints, his parents invested heavily in his education, seeing the promise he had.

Education Against the Odds

Pichai studied Metallurgical Engineering at the prestigious Indian Institute of Technology (IIT) Kharagpur, where he earned a scholarship to Stanford University. The decision was tough—his father spent more than his annual salary just to send Pichai to the US. At Stanford, Pichai lived frugally, often sharing rooms and skipping expensive items to save money.

Early Career in Silicon Valley

After Stanford, Pichai worked at Applied Materials and later earned an MBA from the Wharton School, where he was named a Siebel Scholar and Palmer Scholar for his academic excellence. He joined McKinsey & Company briefly before his life-changing move to Google in 2004.

Joining Google: The Turning Point

At Google, Pichai started with the Google Toolbar project, which allowed users of Internet Explorer and Firefox to access Google easily. This small but strategic project helped increase Google's dominance in search. Later, he led the development of *Google Chrome*, launched in 2008. Chrome became the world's most popular web browser, propelling Pichai into the spotlight.

Rising Through the Ranks

Known for his calm leadership style and vision, Pichai was entrusted with overseeing Gmail, Google Maps, and Android. By 2015, when Google restructured into Alphabet Inc., Pichai was named as the *CEO of Google*. In 2019, he became the *CEO of Alphabet*, overseeing the entire company and its vast range of businesses.

From a Modest Chennai Home to Global Tech Icon

From a boy who grew up without a phone at home to leading one of the most powerful technology companies in the world, Sundar Pichai's story epitomizes the entrepreneurial journey from rags to riches. He is admired for his humility, collaborative leadership, and commitment to innovation.

Legacy and Inspiration

Pichai often shares advice that reflects his journey: *"Wear your failure as a badge of honor and be open to learning."* His life story is a testament to how education, perseverance, and vision can transform even the humblest beginnings into extraordinary success.

Reflection and Workbook: Learning from Global Entrepreneurs

Reading the journeys of *Narayana Murthy, Lakshmi Mittal, Indra Nooyi, Sundar Pichai, Benjamin Franklin, Oprah Winfrey, Walt Disney, Sam Walton, J.K. Rowling,* and *Lucy Guo* can leave us in awe. These stories are inspiring not because these people became wealthy, but because of how they overcame adversity, seized opportunities, and stayed true to their vision. Each of these leaders began with limited resources and faced significant obstacles, yet they transformed challenges into opportunities and built legacies that shaped the world. The true value of their stories lies in what *you* do with them.

To internalize their lessons, take time to reflect and put pen to paper. Now, it's your turn. The following reflections and exercises are designed to help you connect their lessons to your own life. Think of this as the first step in your personal entrepreneurial journey—a space where you translate inspiration into action.

Reflection Questions: From Inspiration to Action

1. Vision Beyond Borders

- If you were not limited by geography, what kind of business would you dream of building?
- How might your idea serve people not just locally, but globally?
- (*Think of Lakshmi Mittal building a global steel empire, or Lucy Guo creating AI companies that scale worldwide.*)

2. Starting Small, Thinking Big

- Murthy began with ₹10,000; Pichai began with a scholarship; Nooyi began with a night job.
- Franklin started as a printer's apprentice; Rowling wrote her first Harry Potter book in cafés while on welfare.
- What is your smallest available resource today, and how could you use it as a starting point?

3. Turning Obstacles into Opportunities

- Mittal saw restrictive policies in India as a reason to expand abroad.
- Oprah transformed childhood poverty and trauma into a drive to inspire millions.
- Disney faced repeated business failures before creating Mickey Mouse.
- What current challenge in your life could actually become a hidden opportunity?

4. Leadership and Integrity

- Which leader's story resonates with you most, and why?

- Sam Walton built Walmart by obsessing over customer value; Sundar Pichai rose through humility and vision; Franklin lived by principles he wrote into his "13 Virtues".
- How would you describe your own leadership style if you were running a team or company?

5. Resilience and Reinvention

- Rowling faced dozens of rejections before publishing her books featuring Harry Potter.
- Lucy Guo dropped out of college, co-founded Scale AI, and went on to become the youngest self-made woman billionaire.
- How do you react when others doubt your ideas? What keeps you moving forward when doors close?

Practical Exercises

1. $250 Startup Challenge

Imagine you only have $250 (like Murthy started small, or Franklin with his printing press). Write down three businesses you could realistically start with that money.

- Example: A digital service, a small resale venture, a creative online product.

2. Global Problem Solver

Identify one global problem (for example, waste, hunger, digital literacy) that bothers you deeply. Brainstorm five ways you could contribute to solving it with limited resources.

(*Think of Pichai expanding internet access, Oprah using media for education, or Guo building AI tools to solve inefficiencies.*)

3. Resilience Map

Think of one personal failure or setback you have faced.

- Write down what you learned from it.
- Then, describe how you could reframe it as preparation for future success.

(*Disney turned bankruptcy into a lesson; Rowling turned rejection into motivation; Oprah turned hardship into strength.*)

4. Your Leadership Role Model

Choose one of the entrepreneurs. Note down three qualities they demonstrated that you want to develop in yourself.

- Example: Pichai's humility, Nooyi's boldness, Murthy's ethics, Mittal's global vision, Walton's frugality, Oprah's empathy, Franklin's discipline, Disney's imagination, Rowling's persistence, Guo's daring.

Mini Workbook Template

Exercises and Notes

1. $250 Startup Challenge: Three Ideas

  i. ....

  ii. ....

  iii. ....

2. Global Problem and Five Solutions

  Problem: ....

    i. ....
    ii. ....
    iii. ....
    iv. ....
    v. ....

3. Resilience Map
Failure/Setback: ....
Lesson Learned: ....
Future Opportunity: ....

4. Leadership Role Model
Chosen Entrepreneur: ....

Three Qualities to Develop:
    i. ....
    ii. ....
    iii. ....

14

The Journey of Innovation

Your Turn to Invent and Build the Future

Throughout the pages of this book, we have traveled through the rich and dynamic world of invention, from the spark of a new idea to the structured methods of transforming it into reality. We've explored the creative mindset that fuels inventors, the disciplined processes that guide innovation, and the protections that safeguard original work through intellectual property rights. We have also examined the critical roles of entrepreneurs and intrapreneurs in turning ideas into viable, scalable solutions—bringing value not only to the market but to society at large.

But invention is only part of the story.

A brilliant idea, no matter how groundbreaking, remains a missed opportunity unless paired with action. And this is where *entrepreneurial effort* becomes indispensable.

> Innovation without execution is imagination.
> Execution without entrepreneurship is limitation.
> But innovation with entrepreneurship? That's transformation.

Entrepreneurship is the engine that drives invention forward. It is the application of initiative, strategy, and persistence to take an idea beyond the drawing board and into the marketplace. The entrepreneur evaluates the feasibility of a concept, identifies the needs it fulfills, and creates a plan to deliver it effectively to those who need it most. Entrepreneurs are not merely inventors; they are builders, risk-takers, visionaries—and sometimes, even revolutionaries.

You've seen how ideas evolve—from identifying problems and brainstorming solutions, to designing prototypes and navigating the complex world of patents. But to *capitalize on your idea*, you must embrace the entrepreneurial process:

- *Validate your concept* by understanding your audience and refining your value proposition.
- *Build a business model* that accounts for cost, pricing, scalability, and sustainability.
- *Protect your intellectual property* through patents, trade secrets, or trademarks.
- *Seek partners and mentors* who can complement your strengths and help you navigate obstacles.
- *Secure funding* through bootstrapping, investors, or licensing deals.
- *Market your invention* with clarity, confidence, and a compelling story.
- *Deliver consistently*, adapt rapidly, and learn continuously.

Some ideas may blossom into full-fledged ventures. Others may find success through licensing or collaboration with established companies. Both paths are valid—and both require entrepreneurial drive.

I've lived this journey myself. From humble beginnings as a curious child repurposing household items, to a decades-long career developing patented innovations across industries, I've learned that invention and entrepreneurship are inseparable allies. My success was not just in conceiving ideas, but in applying the strategic, commercial, and collaborative effort required to bring them to life—and into the hands of users. That's what moved me from being a dreamer to becoming a recognized inventor and intrapreneur.

> My success was not just in conceiving ideas, but in applying the strategic, commercial, and collaborative effort required to bring them to life—and into the hands of users.

The same potential exists in *you*.

Whether you are a student, a professional, a hobbyist, or a retiree, your ideas hold power. You don't need to start with a million dollars or a high-tech lab. You only need a mindset—a willingness to explore, to act, and to persist. The tools and knowledge shared in this book are now part of your toolkit. But tools are only useful when put to work.

As we step into an age defined by rapid technological advancement, artificial intelligence, and global interconnectivity, the future will belong to those who dare to invent it—and who have the courage to build it.

So ask yourself:

What problem are you passionate about solving?
What idea have you been waiting to explore?
What's stopping you from starting now?

Let this not be the final chapter of a book, but the opening paragraph of your next big pursuit—as an inventor, a creator, and an entrepreneur.

You don't have to wait for the future.

You can *create it*.

Because the world doesn't just need more ideas.

It needs *your idea*—brought to life with vision, purpose, and entrepreneurial effort.

About the Author

Charles Kannankeril was born in Kerala, India, where he earned a Bachelor's degree in chemistry. After immigrating to the United States, he completed a Master's degree in organic chemistry at the University of Massachusetts. Though accepted into the university's doctoral program, Charles chose to broaden his technical expertise by pursuing a second Master's degree in engineering, with a focus on plastics, from the same institution.

Charles has accumulated more than three years of teaching experience at academic institutions in both India and the US. He brings over four decades of research and development expertise in the plastics and rubber industries. Throughout his distinguished career, he has held a variety of technical and leadership roles, including as a Development Engineer, Senior Development Engineer, Senior Engineering Fellow, and Director of Research and Development (R&D).

Innovation and invention have defined Charles's journey from the outset. Growing up in a modest environment with limited resources, he learned to improvise, imagine, and innovate from an early age. Rather than lamenting about what he lacked, he trained himself to recreate, adapt, and build with what was available. This mindset of resourcefulness, curiosity, and determination became the foundation of his inventive spirit.

Through self-guided learning and persistent experimentation, Charles developed the mental discipline and creative approach essential for invention. His story is a testament to the power of setting high goals, thinking differently, and embracing failure as a stepping stone toward success. Over the years, he has come to believe that true creativity flourishes in environments where exploration is encouraged, innovation is driven by purpose, and meaningful impact is prioritized over mere profit.

Charles has conceived and documented more than 300 original product and process ideas. His technical expertise spans a wide range of fields, including:

- Cushioning technology (for example, bubble wrap, foam, paper, and on-demand solutions)
- Food packaging innovations (for example, meat trays, absorbent pads, and microbial control systems)
- Medical and healthcare products (for example, inflatable hospital beds, ostomy bags, blood-wipe pads, and biohazard shipping solutions)
- Solar-powered devices
- High-performance polymer and rubber formulations

One of his notable innovations—a high-temperature-resistant rubber tape capable of withstanding up to 3,400°F—was strategically protected as a trade secret rather than through a patent.

Throughout his extensive R&D career, Charles has learned the value of timely problem-solving, customer-focused innovation, and the entrepreneurial mindset needed to bring ideas to life. He has been awarded 86 patents globally—38 in the US and 48 internationally—with an additional 10 patent applications pending. Several of his inventions are also safeguarded through trade secret protection.

In recognition of his significant contributions, Charles was inducted into the Sealed Air Corporation Inventors Hall of Fame in 2004 and was honored with the Engineer of the Year Award by the Indian Engineers' Association in 2012.

Although he officially retired in 2017, Charles continues to innovate, mentor, and explore new opportunities. His drive is fueled not just by the excitement of discovery, but by the desire to create meaningful change through practical innovation.

In 2018, Charles published his first book, *The Inventor in You: A Step-by-Step Guide to Your First Invention,* which offers practical guidance on identifying problems, developing solutions, transforming those solutions into inventions, and protecting intellectual property.

In this new book, his focus shifts toward helping inventors and creators capitalize on their ideas, inventions, and innovations. He explores strategic pathways such as selling or licensing intellectual property, joining a business as an intrapreneur, or launching a venture as an entrepreneur. Through clear guidance and real-world insights, Charles aims to empower readers to not only invent—but also to bring their innovations to the market and generate a lasting impact.

By sharing his life and research experiences, Charles' goal is to inspire readers to be creative, set ambitious goals, and make meaningful contributions to society by building a better, more innovative world.